From Lullabies to Literature

Stories in the Lives of Infants and Toddlers

Jennifer Birckmayer,
Anne Kennedy,
and Anne Stonehouse

National Association for the Education of Young Children
Washington, DC, USA

Pademelon Press

Pademelon Press, Castle Hill, NSW, Australia

National Association for
the Education of
Young Children
1313 L Street NW, Suite 500
Washington, DC 20005-4101
202-232-8777 • 800-424-2460
www.naeyc.org

NAEYC Books
Director, Publications and
Educational Initiatives
Carol Copple

Managing Editor
Bry Pollack

Design and Production
Malini Dominey

Editorial Associate
Cassandra Berman

Editorial Associate
Melissa Edwards

Permissions
Lacy Thompson

Marketing Director
Matt Munroe

Through its publications program, the National Association for the Education of Young Children (NAEYC) provides a forum for discussion of major issues and ideas in the early childhood field, with the hope of provoking thought and promoting professional growth. The views expressed or implied in this book are not necessarily those of the Association or its members.

Permissions

Excerpt from *The Power of Observation, 2d ed.* (p. 64), by J.R. Jablon, A.L. Dombro, and M.L. Dichtelmiller (Washington, DC: Teaching Strategies, Inc. and NAEYC, 2007), is reprinted by permission. Copyright 2007 by J.R. Jablon, A.L. Dombro, and M.L. Dichtelmiller.

Credits

Collage artwork by Sandi Collins, copyright © 2008 NAEYC. Developmental editing: Susan A. Liddicoat

A copublication of the National Association for the Education of Young Children, 1313 L Street NW, Suite 500, Washington, DC 20005-4101, USA; and Pademelon Press Pty. Ltd., 7/3 Packard Avenue, Castle Hill, NSW 2154, Australia.

Library of Congress Control Number: 2008928173
ISBN: 978-1-928896-52-4
NAEYC Item #2010

Meet the Authors

We are three authors from very different places, but we share extensive professional and personal experiences of working with and enjoying the company of infants and toddlers. You could say we are passionate about very young children's remarkable competencies and enthusiasm for learning about themselves and their world. As readers and storytellers in our professional and personal lives, we also share a passion and deep interest in stories and storytelling. We have all worked in child care services, as trainers for services, and in colleges and universities, in the United States and in Australia. Inevitably and gratefully, we have learned from the dedicated teachers, child care providers, students, parents, and children with whom we have worked.

Jennifer Birckmayer has been an early childhood educator, speaker, lecturer, and author for more than forty years. She recently retired from her position as senior extension associate for the Department of Human Development at Cornell University (New York, USA). She is a consultant/trainer for Libraries for the Future, Family Place Libraries, and the State University of New York Early Childhood Training Strategies Group. Among her publications are *Bookstart* (with B.J. Westendorf) and *Discipline Is Not a Dirty Word.*

Anne Kennedy has worked in the field of early childhood education for more than thirty years as a teacher and child care director and also as a teacher educator at Monash University (Melbourne, Australia). Dr. Kennedy's research and publications have focused mainly on ethics in early childhood education and early literacy. She is currently the chairperson of Community Childcare Victoria, which represents community-owned children's services, including long day care, family child care, and out of school hours care.

Anne Stonehouse is an early childhood education leader in both the United States and Australia. She has worked for more than thirty-five years as a trainer, academic, consultant, conference speaker, and writer. She has authored a number of publications, including *Prime Times* (with J. Greenman and G. Schweikert) and *Making Links* (with J. Gonzalez-Mena). In 1999 she was made a Member of the Order of Australia, an honor that recognized her outstanding contributions to early childhood education in Australia and beyond.

Contents

About This Book

This is a book about sharing stories with infants and toddlers. Our premise in writing it is that we want every young child to discover the richness, power, and pleasure of language as it is spoken, sung, and printed. For children to make this discovery, they need to be in close relationships with sensitive and loving adults who understand the unique characteristics and development of infants and toddlers, while respecting the wide range of individual differences within these age groups. Sharing stories with children can nourish those kinds of relationships.

Child care providers, teachers, parents, older siblings, grandparents, and others who care for or about young children all have roles to play in introducing children under the age of 3 to the delights of language. Although we hope to be helpful to them in providing practical suggestions, this is not a "how-to-do-it" book. Neither is it a scholarly summary and analysis of research, though we do include select research-based findings. Instead, we aim to present ideas for reflection and discussion.

Why this book is needed

The first reason we think a book about sharing stories with infants and toddlers is needed is the notion of "emergent literacy" (Sulzby & Teale 1991; Purcell-Gates 1996; Clay 2001)—by which we mean the constellation of skills and attitudes children accumulate related to reading and writing before they are ready for formal instruction. Brain research has highlighted the importance of children's early years for their learning and later success in school and life.

Explaining emerging literacy to families

The public focus on literacy has made many families anxious about their children's progress in this area. They may be unsure about what they and their children's caregivers should be doing to support literacy development and learning. Caregivers can reassure families that sharing stories and talking with their child as a part of everyday life is the best way to nurture literacy and provide the foundation for future literacy development.

Often family members will ask caregivers about some of their practices. In the case of literacy learning, a parent in a group of older toddlers may ask, for example, "Why aren't you teaching children to recognize letters of the alphabet?" When caregivers have a good understanding of the reasons for the experiences they offer (and don't offer!) and the many ways those experiences support literacy learning, they can answer such questions convincingly and to families' satisfaction.

In high-quality early childhood care and education programs, families and caregivers always work in partnership or collaboration, communicating openly and sharing information and perspectives about the child and the child's care experience.

As often happens, a plethora of products in the marketplace has resulted—books for children, books for adults, resource kits, videos, and software—all targeting experiences during children's first three years. Evaluating the range of approaches and recommendations can be confusing for caregivers and families. All the products promote themselves as being important, even essential, for children's learning and specifically for their literacy development. But the often-used slogan "literacy begins at birth" is interpreted in many different ways, some more appropriate than others. Worse still, adoption of some of these recommendations—among them, highly structured, adult-directed activities and watered-down versions of activities suitable for older children—is not in very young children's best interests.

Another need that this book fills is providing insights to the infant/toddler caregiver who works effectively but intuitively—that is, without being fully aware of the impact of the experiences, interactions, and environments she or he provides. The use of stories with children of this age is a good example. As we demonstrate, when we are more intentional about sharing stories, either in planned or spontaneous experiences but always with full awareness of their benefits, children gain much more from the story experience. Caregivers also have the satisfaction of knowing that they are giving children something not just enjoyable but also very valuable.

Finally, this book addresses the stubborn misconception that "physical and neurological maturation alone prepare the child to take advantage of [literacy] instruction, . . . [so] until children reach a certain stage of maturity, all exposure to [literacy experiences] . . . is a waste of time or even potentially harmful" (Neuman, Copple, & Bredekamp 2000, 4–5). Often, caregivers who think this way will offer infants and toddlers few or no story experiences, believing that stories don't matter yet or that fostering the foundational skills necessary for literacy is a job for teachers of older children. They are wrong on both counts (see, e.g., Bredekamp & Copple 1997; Neuman, Copple, & Bredekamp 2000).

What's special about this book

There are many excellent books on the topics of early language, literacy, and children's literature (e.g., Butler 1998; Jalongo 2004; Makin & Whitehead 2004; Bardige & Segal 2005). So what makes this book different?

1. Very few of the books on early language and literacy and children's literature focus entirely on children younger than 3 years old, as this book does.

2. Instead of using a narrow definition of "literacy" (i.e., the ability to read and write and to comprehend and use what is read or written), we take a perspective that focuses on the power of stories.

3. Our definition of "stories" is unique. For example, what an adult might say when looking with an infant at pictures in a simple concept book is often a very simple story by our definition: "That's a cow. The cow says, 'Moo.' Cows like to eat grass."

4. The benefits of sharing stories are looked at broadly. Our book covers the ways stories can enrich children's lives, support and strengthen relationships, and help to lay the foundations for early literacy.

5. We put considerable emphasis on caregivers and families learning *from each other*, as well as on the ways that, through working together, they can increase the joys and benefits of sharing stories with young children.

6. This book is the product of a bicultural (Australian-American) perspective.

Beyond birth to 3

Although our focus in this book is on children under 3 years of age, much of the content applies to older children as well, particularly those who are challenged in the areas of language and communication. And, although our audience is adults who work with children in early childhood care and education programs, both home- and center-based, much of the content applies to any adult who interacts with children under 3 in any setting, including a parent and child at home.

Overview of the chapters

The broad definition of "stories" adopted for this book is explained in **Chapter 1,** where also the case is made for stories' value in enriching very young children's lives, strengthening relationships, and supporting their literacy development.

The starting point for interacting meaningfully with children is knowing them—both individually and generally as an age group possessing typical behaviors, interests, and abilities. In **Chapter 2,** we present important aspects of infant and toddler development, with a focus on language and literacy.

Chapter 3 focuses on the use of language in conversations, simple storytelling, and language games with children from birth on, as well as ways to build stories naturally into children's experiences. **Chapter 4** gives a rationale for the special place of books in an early childhood program, describes types of books, and suggests some criteria for building or adding to a book collection. **Chapter 5** focuses on the effective use of stories and books.

Chapter 6 considers the place of stories in program planning. Partnering with families is the focus for **Chapter 7,** as caregivers and families provide better experiences for children when they work in collaboration. **Chapter 8** concludes the book by revisiting the three benefits of story sharing and reminding readers of the importance of giving every infant and toddler the opportunity to share in stories of all kinds.

Special features

Two special features appear throughout the book:

Discussion Starters. These are distributed throughout the book and are intended to help readers think about and discuss information and issues with colleagues or classmates. The Discussion Starters can also help connect the content in the chapters with caregiving work.

Recommended children's books. In the chapters, we mention or reference some of the many, many good books available for infants and toddlers. A deliberate attempt has been made to include old classics as well as newer books for children ages 3 and under. We hope that some of the older books will elicit good memories in the reader. All of the children's books mentioned are listed in the Appendix, along with select other children's books of value. The list of books is designed to guide readers who may be unsure about which books are appropriate for very young children.

Our aim for readers

In summary, our aim in writing this book is that it will be a guide for practice and a basis for reflection and discussion. After reading and thinking about its content and challenges, we hope that readers will:

- feel affirmed as storytellers and be clear about the place of stories in the lives of very young children;
- continue to use stories enthusiastically and joyfully, or discover for the first time the delights of doing so;
- work with a deeper understanding of the potential of stories to enrich the lives of infants and toddlers, strengthen relationships, and support the development of literacy skills and understandings; and
- support families' use of stories with their children at home, and encourage family members to share personal stories with the adults who care for their children.

"The Captain's on deck, waltzing in time . . . Hey ho, little fish. Good night, goo

Why Stories Matter

The Joys and Benefits for Infants and Toddlers

We tell stories because we must. Stories are what make us human.
—Arnold Zable, *The Fig Tree*

As the Australian author Arnold Zable says, whether we are young or old, stories connect us and add meaning to our lives. For generations, stories have been a way we share information and ideas. They are occasions for us to connect emotionally and to explore and express hopes and fears. Stories are something to listen to, watch, or read; something to tell, sing, draw, or write. For very young children especially, stories are occasions for relationship building through closeness, interaction, and sharing. They provide an opportunity for gaining skills and concepts across all domains, especially the language skills necessary for literacy and the concept of what reading and writing are. To build their sense of self, construct an understanding of the world around them, and take the first steps toward literacy, young children *need* to hear stories and to tell stories.

The definition of stories here may be labeled by some as quirky, by others as too broad, and by many as unconventional. This book is premised on the belief that there is a wide range of experiences we want to call "sharing stories" that begin at birth and are meaningful in the lives of very young children. *From Lullabies to Literature*, the title of this book, aims to convey the variety of these experiences. When adults and children share stories, whatever the child's age, the benefits are many: relationships are strengthened, language is learned, literacy skills are introduced, new ideas are explored, skills are developed, feelings are communicated, and most important, the child and adult are having fun together.

What do we mean by "stories"?

As usually defined, a "story" is a recounting of events, either real or imaginary, set in the past, the present, or the future. An ordinary, everyday conversation with a young child might include a story. For example, Maria tells a simple story when she says to several toddlers as they run inside out of the rain:

> "Remember how it rained really hard last week, and when it stopped, we went outside, walked in the puddles, and saw a beautiful rainbow in the sky? Then we came in and made a big picture of a rainbow."

Stories
can be
told or
written,
heard
or read.

A more complex story would have a beginning, middle, and end, as well as characters, chronology, and settings. Stories can be told or written, heard or read. Stories can take the form of prose, poem, picture, rhyme, chant, or song. Some stories are informal and private, created and shared as children and adults go about their daily lives. Other stories are formal and public, published as books or presented in other forms of media to large audiences.

This book about the joys and benefits of sharing stories with infants and toddlers defines "story" even more broadly to also include story experiences that are not much more than "events plus emotion." For example, by that definition, this family child care provider is telling a simple story to the infant she is dressing:

> "I'm putting on your shirt! I'm putting on your pants! I'm putting on your hat! Now off we go to the park!" Her smiling face and tone of voice let him know something good is happening, and he participates in the story by smiling back.

Supporting this broad conception of "stories" are early language experiences that are precursors to the skills and understandings children need to become story participants in more conventional ways. Examples for infants and toddlers include making, listening to, and reacting to sounds and also engaging in spoken language experiences such as conversations and face, lap, and knee games.

From Lullabies to Literature

While stories might be more often associated with children older than infants and toddlers, the following examples are a reminder of their attraction for very young children:

> Eight-month-old Myra smiles happily, puts her thumb into her mouth, and looks and listens intently as her caregiver recites a familiar nursery rhyme. She makes an effort to imitate the gestures that go along with it.

> At 18 months of age, Kayla has favorites among the books in her family child care library. Today she has chosen a book about "things that go" and looks intently at the page with the moving van. Her caregiver sees her looking and says, "That's like the van that came to your house last week. The movers put all your things and your mum's and dad's things in the truck and took them to your new house. And now you're living in a brand new house with your own room."

> Nicky, 32 months old, frequently asks his parents to "tell me the story about when I was born."

The mode of the storytelling will change as the child develops and learns. For the youngest children, pictures accompanying oral storytelling are important, and children gradually learn that the narrative is telling a story about the images; then later, children also can interact with text. As children grow, the previous modes aren't abandoned; the new ones are just added into children's story repertoires.

In high-quality settings, caregivers carefully plan a sequence of experiences that fit what children are like, what interests them, and what they can do. This applies to sharing stories, too. To be effective, experiences with sounds, language, storytelling, and books aren't just offered randomly. Different story experiences are appropriate at different times, and certain experiences lay the groundwork for later ones. While the emphasis should always be on knowing children's interests and ensuring that interactions and communication are warm, engaging, and appropriate, attention to the many changes that children undergo in the first three years of life, and the implications of these for the kinds of story experiences offered, is important.

What do we mean by "sharing stories"?

The term *sharing* is used very broadly in this book to refer to all the ways caregivers make sure that infants and toddlers are exposed to "stories" as we have defined them. For our purposes, sharing encompasses:

- Telling children informal simple stories in everyday conversations—stories about what has happened, what is happening, and what is going to happen.
- Singing and listening to songs together, and encouraging children to really listen.
- Telling children stories that are part of the oral tradition—the myths, fables, and tales that have been told and retold for generations.
- Encouraging children to tell stories, and writing down the stories they tell.
- Supporting the beginnings of children's own story making through their dramatic or pretend play.
- Sitting with one child or a couple of children with a book; looking at and talking about the pictures together.
- Using pictures in a book to tell children a story independent of printed text.
- Reading a book with a child.
- Providing a variety of appropriate books for children to use independently.

Why do stories matter for very young children?

When stories are part of children's lives from birth, the children benefit in three important ways. Overlapping considerably, these benefits are that stories *enrich children's lives*, *strengthen relationships*, and *support their emerging literacy*. Each of these benefits is described below and then highlighted throughout the book.

How do stories enrich children's lives?

Stories can reflect past experience, expand what is happening in the present, and give clues about the future. With help from sensitive and skilled adults, through stories very young children can:

Access information—For example, discovering the sounds various animals make and what they eat; why the wind blows; what other people do, think, and feel.

Learn new concepts—For example, a young child's experience with cats may be limited to one visit with her neighbor's pet, but a book about their different colors, shapes, and sizes can increase her awareness and expand her original concept of what "cat" means.

Learn to wonder and ask questions, and have the satisfaction of getting answers to their questions—For example, guessing when the adult says, "And what do you think happened next?"

Experience the rhythms, rhymes, and beauty of language—For example, e.e. cummings's description of spring as "when the world is mud-luscious . . . and puddle-wonderful" illustrates the power of beautiful language.

> Ella, an almost 3-year-old, reflects her familiarity with nursery rhymes when she looks out the window on a rainy day and chants, "One misty, moisty morning."

Reflect on and clarify past experiences, and link them to the present—For example, a recent trip to a farm comes alive again when a story is shared about all the animals in the barn.

Anticipate experiences that lie ahead—For example, a story about infants can be a link for a child who will soon have a baby brother or sister. Such stories are an important tool in helping children establish a sense of confidence and competence to cope with challenges and new events.

Become informed about experiences they may not have had—For example, children may learn about visiting the zoo, going to the hospital, or moving to a new home. Stories used in this way enable adults to tailor explanations of unfamiliar events to the individual needs and interests of a child.

See a reflection of themselves and their experiences—For example, a toddler who shouts, "Just like me!" when he hears or sees a child in a story doing something familiar is expressing a rush of recognition that even adults still sometimes experience in a story that hits home with them.

Be lifted out of the tedium of daily routines, or escape when reality is too unpleasant—Just as adults may turn to a favorite poem, prayer, or book for comfort or to lighten a mood, so can young children learn to use stories in self-soothing ways.

Imagine—For example, after hearing a story about Winnie the Pooh, a child might imagine that his own stuffed animals play amongst themselves. Stories can stimulate and expand children's ability to think beyond what they know in their everyday lives.

Have fun—Funny stories make children laugh. Even combinations of silly sounds, like "Knick-knack paddywhack," can catch an infant's attention and elicit a smile.

Language play

Well-chosen stories offer delightful ways to play with language through rhyme, repetition, humor, and imaginative combinations of words, themes, characters, and settings.

The language of stories often includes words or phrases that people do not use in everyday conversations. This helps children build their vocabularies, and they frequently reveal in quaint and startling ways their knowledge of a word or phrase that adults might not expect them to know. Here's a classic example of unique expressions children might learn by interacting with stories:

> Jack and Jill went up the hill to fetch a pail of water.
> Jack fell down and broke his crown and Jill came tumbling after.
> Up Jack got and home did trot as fast as he could caper.
> He went to bed and fixed his head with vinegar and brown paper.

Most American or Australian children today would be unfamiliar with many of this nursery rhyme's words and phrases, such as *crown* for head or "fetch a pail." Still, the plot, characters, and rhythm of the story have interested many generations of children. Infants may not understand any of the words but will be entranced by the rhythm of the language and the excitement and enthusiasm of the adult who recites it.

Thus, a simple story may portray or expand upon the child's actual experience, and the adult can bring out familiar details while at the same time making the variations part of an interesting and absorbing story. Children learn from repetition of familiar themes, gaining a sense of confidence, which gently leads them to explore new ideas and more elaborate stories.

How do stories strengthen relationships?

Stories are powerful tools for communicating and interacting with young children. As such, they can strengthen children's relationships with adults and with other children. Experts in brain research confirm that warm, loving, and consistent relationships with adults are essential for healthy brain development in young children (Shore 1997; McCain & Mustard 1999; Shonkoff & Phillips 2000; Lally & Mangione 2006).

Both the act of telling or reading stories and their content can make these relationships stronger and deeper. Stories can be vehicles for conversations, relaxed closeness between an adult and a child, and a mutual enjoyment of shared experiences, all of which contribute to the special bonds that are so important.

Stories can strengthen relationships by:

Helping children learn about the values and beliefs of their families and cultures. For example, the story in a book such as *Feast for 10*, by Catherine Falwell, depicts a family in which parents believe that the children can help with grocery shopping and preparing a meal.

Exposing children to emotions similar to their own, and helping them explore feelings and label them. For example, hearing a story about a boy who worries about spending the night at his grandma's house might help a child identify that it's natural to feel "nervous" about sleeping in an unfamiliar bedroom.

Allowing children to connect with and learn from the lives and experiences of others. Over the first three years of life, children become increasingly interested in other children, other members of their families, and the affairs and events of everyday life. Hearing about the experiences of other people can reassure a child about the universal nature of her own experiences and foster a sense of connection with all other human beings.

Increasing awareness of the differences among people. As children learn about cultural and other kinds of differences and the reasons for them, they can be encouraged to develop attitudes of acceptance and interest in not only people who are like them but also people who look different and live different lives.

Adding to appreciation of the basic similarities that lie beneath more obvious differences. When we say to a child, "Did I tell you the story about when I . . . " or "Let me tell you about what happened when . . . " we are using personal stories to connect our lives with others. Stories can cross the borders of time and place better than many other experiences because they connect children and adults to each other through the sharing of universal feelings and experiences.

In addition to supporting close, strong relationships between young children and their caregivers, stories also offer a focus for communication and positive interactions between caregivers and families and a means to strengthen relationships between them. For example, caregivers can encourage family members to share stories not only with their child at home but also with other children as part of the program. This can be a wonderful way for the program to show respect for and interest in cultural and linguistic diversity and is likely to enrich the program for everyone. Books and other materials can be made available to families to encourage and assist their storytelling. (The use of stories to promote partnerships with families is the topic of Chapter 7.)

Sharing stories can also help children establish and sustain relationships with each other. Toddlers who share in story experiences with other toddlers learn that they have many of the same needs, feelings, and interests.

How do stories support literacy development?

There are many different definitions of literacy, but no matter which one is adopted, sharing stories strongly contributes to children's emerging learning and development. One definition that fits comfortably with the contents of this book comes from the Early Childhood Australia position statement on language and literacy (1999): "Literacy can be seen as language in use—in speaking, listening, reading, viewing, writing, and drawing. What is involved in each of these language modes varies according to context, purpose, and audience." NAEYC states that "literacy learning begins at birth and is encouraged through participation with adults in meaningful activities; these literacy behaviors change and eventually become conventional over time" (Neuman, Copple, & Bredekamp 2000, 123).

Literacy and community

Drawing on the statements above, we can say that literacy is a social and cultural practice that involves a number of skills and understandings. Every day very young children are immersed in the literacy events that occur in their homes and communities, including child care programs. These practices and events are valued and therefore regarded as important for children to learn about and participate in actively. Some communities will have a strong emphasis on oral literacy skills or on being able to "read" people's body language or gestures. In Australia, Indigenous children living in remote communities need to learn how to "read" the signs and sounds of the land to develop survival skills in what is often a harsh environment. Similarly, a toddler from a Spanish-speaking family in New York City learns quickly to identify picture symbols for bus and train stations, ice cream shops, and pizza parlors.

All children, including those with special needs, are able to participate in literacy events such as stories. For some children, different strategies and additional resources will be required to support that process. Caregivers working with older children with special needs may find that some of the experiences recommended in this book are appropriate for them.

The power of stories and books

Early literacy abilities develop as infants first listen, recognize, and then gradually use sounds, gestures, and later words, written marks, or drawings to communicate their needs, wants, feelings, and thoughts in ways appropriate to the practices of their communities. The role of adults is to listen, respond, and talk naturally and respectfully about these efforts. Toddlers become increasingly competent communicators as they play and participate in everyday events with adults and peers and learn the power of words and gestures to convey meaning and to interpret their understandings to others.

As children listen to stories, they learn much about the purpose of telling stories and the routines for their use. For example, hearing a particular tone of voice or a phrase such as "Once upon a time . . . " or "Who wants to listen to a story?" lets children know that what is about to be shared with them differs from a conversation. From stories children learn about "book language" and how this may be different from everyday language (Armbruster, Lehr, & Osborn 2003). Very young children can learn to listen carefully as a story is told or read. Learning to be a good listener—to pay attention to a story— helps children to learn to follow a character, theme, or plot, which links to becoming a reader.

When we share stories with very young children, they are not yet capable of interpreting the written words or letters on the page, and yet they can enjoy the story. Even at a very young age, children can show us that they understand what we are telling or reading to them. All books shared with infants and toddlers, whether traditional story books or not, can be the prompt or catalyst for a story. These days, there are a great number of books to choose from that have been written especially for this age group. Books expose children to the power, pleasure, rhythm, and richness of language and can be introduced to children in their infancy.

Children "read" pictures before they read words. Some writers use the phrase "reading the visual" to refer to the ability to make meaning from pictures (Anstey & Bull 2000). This, by the way, is one of the reasons that the pictures or illustrations in children's books need to be clear, accurate, and closely reflective of the text. Children learn that they can be involved with stories through pointing at pictures, asking or answering questions, or joining in on a repetitive line such as "Run, run, run as fast as you can. You can't catch me, I'm the gingerbread man."

Gradually very young children become aware of the printed words in books and begin to understand that the written symbols are important for

> Children "read" pictures before they read words.

conveying a message. By experiencing through observation and interactions with adults and other children how print, signs, and symbols in the environment work, a very young child gradually understands their power and importance and begins to use them in play and drawings (Parlakian 2003; Jalongo 2004).

While children have a strong innate propensity for oral language development, literacy development is more dependent on experience. That is one of the important reasons why every child needs to experience stories (Centre for Community Child Health 2004). Infants and toddlers have the ability and the need to participate in literacy events, or "language in use." Listening to language in stories, being captivated by its beauty, learning what words mean, being encouraged to use language, and seeing it in print are important beginnings in literacy that cultivate children's interest. Stories of all types—written, viewed, or told—are the most powerful and appropriate way to support this age group in their language and literacy development and learning.

Discussion Starter

How will you explain the benefits of sharing stories to a colleague or parent of a very young child in your care? Write brief notes to yourself about your responses to the following:

1. How does sharing stories enrich children's lives?
2. How can sharing stories strengthen relationships between adults and children? among children? among adults?
3. How does sharing stories foster emerging literacy skills in very young children?
4. Can you think of additional benefits of using stories with very young children?

Stories, broadly defined, contribute in significant ways to children's lives. They help children learn about other people, themselves, and the world around them. The dramatic changes that occur in children in the first three years of life have implications for the use of stories and the kinds of stories shared. The next chapter focuses on the characteristics of infants and toddlers that impact how to best share stories with them.

From Lullabies to Literature

"This little piggy went to the market" . . . Where's Jack's toe? Is this your toe, Jack? Yes, that's Jack's

About Very Young Children
Typical Early Abilities and Development

Read to me. My story is just beginning.
—banner in a supermarket

Between birth and age 3, children make enormous strides in development, more rapid and dramatic than at any other period in their lives. Even a few months can make a big difference in the skills and interests of an infant or toddler as a story participant. The following vignette only hints at the breathtaking changes that can occur:

> At 11 months, Chloe is a happy, busy child. She enjoys crawling to the bookshelf and pulling all the books out onto the floor. Occasionally she allows her caregiver to show her a page from one of the books, but her interest is brief. By 14 months, however, Chloe is walking, if unsteadily, and can say several words.
>
> Her interest in stories has changed, too. She brings books to share with her caregiver several times a day. She enjoys face, hand, and lap games and listens carefully when her caregiver recites nursery rhymes, talks about pictures, and tells simple stories. Chloe particularly enjoys "Baa, Baa, Black Sheep," even *baa*-ing along enthusiastically—and whenever she sees a picture of a sheep!

As children change, the stories we share with them and they share with us will change, too. This chapter highlights the characteristics and developmental trajectory typical of children over their first three years, including the variability and diversity among children and families that make sharing stories with the very young both challenging and so rewarding.

An image of infants and toddlers

Our general understanding, or mental image, of very young children not only affects how we interact with them but also influences the experiences we as caregivers provide—the ways we talk and listen, the stories we tell, and the books we share. But how accurate is our image? The following compilation of characteristics, based on both brain research and professional experience with infants and toddlers, is the foundation for the approaches and practices advocated in this book. Reminding ourselves what infants and toddlers are really like and what they are able to do can only make the story experiences we share more beneficial to them and our interactions more meaningful.

Both being and becoming

It is easy to fall into the trap of seeing very young children only in terms of their potential, as *becoming* people rather than already *being* people who deserve to be understood for who they currently are, not just for who they will someday be. Accepting that children are currently *being* means that the experiences you provide for them—both story experiences and otherwise—must address who they are now *and* lay the groundwork for their future learning and development.

Throughout this book, there is emphasis on the range of children's individual interest levels in stories, even among children of the same age. Though each child will develop preferences for certain stories and even how to interact with them (e.g., pointing at pictures in a book, flipping pages very quickly), it is important to expose all children to a variety of stories and methods of experiencing stories, both familiar and new. Doing this supports both being and becoming.

For example, some older toddlers learn to read some words, and a few learn to read. Many toddlers show awareness that pictures and printed words convey meaning. While we would never push the development of these emerging literacy skills through drills or lessons, we also would never discourage or stop a toddler who wants to learn to read. Responding to a demonstrated interest is different from pushing a child; we always want to let the child's own preferences and interests be our guide.

Many toddlers show awareness that pictures and printed words convey meaning.

Ready to develop relationships and communicate

Infants are ready for relationships from birth (Hawley 2000). They initiate interactions with other people very early in their lives, and long before they can understand what others are saying or express themselves in words, they respond to human voices, particularly the voices of those they know and love. As they develop, infants play increasingly active roles in establishing and strengthening relationships.

Infants are also competent communicators. Before they can speak, they use and imitate body language, including facial expressions (Barton & Brophy-Herb 2006). Anyone working with infants and toddlers is familiar with their efforts to get their messages across, even when their language skills are not very developed: An insistent tug on the arm, a sloppy kiss, or a cry of fright are just a few of the communication strategies that we encounter and interpret when we work with very young children.

When we share stories with very young children, their individual responses are often very different from what we expect. Sometimes they communicate their lack of interest by closing their eyes, turning or walking away, interrupting, or demanding a different story. Or conversely, they may join in, shouting enthusiastic comments and suggestions, while at other times they are simply still and attentive. Our acknowledgement of these responses is crucial if children are to see themselves as competent communicators, able eventually to become storytellers themselves. And when we listen to their stories, we model attentiveness and reinforce children's willingness to listen carefully when others share stories with them.

Competent

Though young children are dependent upon adults, they are not helpless. Anyone working with young children is sometimes amazed by what they can grasp—as long as we pay more attention to what infants and toddlers *can* do than to what they cannot (Parlakian 2003; Barton & Brophy-Herb 2006).

For example, consider the depth of this toddler's understanding that symbols have meaning and also his persistence in conveying his question:

> Sixteen-month-old Noah points and says the same thing over and over again whenever he looks at a decorative plaque in his family child care home. Despite Noah's efforts, his caregiver can't understand what he is trying to say; neither can his parents. But one day when his grandma picks him up, she finally is able to translate Noah's words as "What say?" When she replies, "Noah, this says,

'Home is where the heart is,'" he beams at her. His question is *finally* answered!

Very young children are learning to extract meaning from their environments and make connections between new and familiar things. Sharing stories is one of the best ways to discover just how aware of their surroundings young children can be. Here, toddler Jai is more observant than his caregiver Gina realizes:

> As Gina and Jai share a book, Jai points to one of the pictures—a boy in a red jacket—and announces emphatically, "Daddy!" Gina wonders if Jai is still calling all males "Daddy" at 29 months. She responds, "Do you think that boy looks like your daddy? He has blond hair, but your daddy's hair is black." At the end of the day, however, the connection is clear: Jai's father comes to pick him up wearing a new red jacket!

Another piece of evidence that children have a remarkable level of cognitive competence is their capability to learn more than one language with relative ease. Researchers looking at early language development in one, two, or more languages find that humans inherit the capacity to communicate in different ways, and children are very clever at doing this from birth (Papadaki-D'Onofrio 2003; Long & Volk 2004; Jones-Diaz & Harvey 2007).

Full of zest for learning

Infants and toddlers have enormous, contagious (although sometimes exhausting!) enthusiasm for learning. They seize every possible opportunity to explore, discover, and figure out the world surrounding them. Very young children learn all the time, not just during planned learning activities. They can find something interesting in the most ordinary situations and with the most ordinary materials.

Active construction

From birth on, children play a major role in their own development and learning, as active constructors of their own understandings from their daily experiences (Bredekamp & Copple 1997; Bowman 2004). Those experiences include a young child's firsthand observation and exploration of the world. They also include sharing knowledge among children and adults, during which each side makes a contribution to the experience or interaction, impacting what happens next through their responses. For example:

Supporting language diversity

Families often have questions about first- and second-language acquisition and maintenance. Learning a second language is dependent on the level of development in the first language, which means that infants and toddlers need to be supported in becoming competent in their home language (Siraj-Blatchford & Clarke 2000; Gregory & Kenner 2003). Sharing stories and other language experiences can help with that. For example, caregivers can:

• Encourage families to maintain their child's first language in the home by sharing stories there.

• Share stories in the classroom using the child's home language, if caregivers are themselves bilingual or bicultural.

• Learn and use key words such as *hello* or *yes* in the child's home language.

• Ask families to record their child's favorite songs or stories in the home language, so these can be used in the program.

• Have a range of books and print examples in the classroom that use children's home languages.

Learning two languages is a rich cognitive, social, and cultural resource for individual children and for groups of children. Caregivers who respect and value young children's right to maintain their first language can play an important role in supporting them through the use of shared stories in that language.

Fourteen-month-old Santiago says, "Apple!" enthusiastically when his caregiver Molly talks to him about their day. Though Santiago's speech is limited, he makes an important contribution to the story of the time they have spent together. Molly replies, "Yes, we did have apples for this morning's snack! You liked the apples, didn't you? I wonder what we will have for snack this afternoon. Let's go and see."

Santiago remembers that he enjoyed his morning snack, and his reminding Molly about it directs the course of their conversation.

Very young children's learning is enhanced by the presence and participation of a thoughtful adult. Sharing stories can exemplify this partnership in learning:

Several times during the day, Shaina, one of the toddlers in Mark's classroom, takes his hand and pulls him to a row of photographs on display near the cubbies. She points to a photo of herself and her older brother and says to Mark, "Tell!" Mark obliges with a quick story about what Shaina and her big brother do together at home.

Hands-on

Learning for very young children is hands-on—so much so that it may be more accurately described as "bodies-on"! In their quest to learn, they mostly want experiences that allow them to get physically involved. They are not likely to sit still and simply watch and listen. Very young children's interactions with stories are no exception: For example, adults may be used to simply looking at and reading books, but for toddlers, books are also objects to grab, chew, flap, and carry around the room. Telling a story that involves movements for children to imitate or that allows them to chime in with a repetitive phrase is likely to capture their interest and support their need to be active participants in a story experience (Jalongo 2004).

Unpredictable focus

Often very young children's drive to find out, to figure out, and to explore their interests—in just about everything—can get in the way of their focusing for a long time on one thing. Anyone who cares for infants and toddlers has had experiences to suggest they have short attention spans, as when we are in the midst of telling what we think is an engrossing story, only to have our audience wander off to check out something new.

However, it is more accurate to describe very young children's attention spans as unpredictable. Many times we are surprised by what *does* capture children's interest, and for considerable periods of time, such as turning the pages of a board book for ten minutes or more, all the while ignoring its contents. An older infant might seem never to tire of face and lap games and not ever to be interested in books. Or one day a toddler might sit in rapt attention while his caregiver tells a familiar story, whereas the previous day that toddler wasn't interested in the story at all. Even a catalogue from a hardware store might capture a child's attention, while a board book designed especially for her age group is tossed aside without a second glance.

Discussion Starter

1. What other characteristics would you add to this image of very young children? How do they relate to sharing stories?
2. Have you seen examples of these characteristics in your interactions with very young children?

From Lullabies to Literature

Influenced by multiple contexts

Children live in and are influenced by multiple contexts (family, community, culture, biology, etc.), only one of which is their child care setting (Bronfenbrenner 1979; Rogoff 2003). From birth, there is an interaction between each child and all these contexts. The contexts have their impact both through intrinsic variables, such as ability, temperament, interest, and styles of learning, and through extrinsic variables, such as socioeconomic status, family structure, and language(s) spoken; parents' age, level of education, and occupation; and background experiences. It is the intersection of all those variables that make young children so diverse. Consider these two 18-month-olds:

> Lucia's family recently immigrated from Mexico to a small town in the United States, where they have moved in with her father's cousin and his four older children. Lucia is the much-loved baby of her large extended family. A relative is always available to carry, sing to, and play with her. She is unfamiliar with books, but loves to clap her hands and sway when her caregiver sings familiar songs with her in Spanish.

> Ronnie lives in a small apartment in a big city with his young single mother, Sonia. While Sonia works hard during the day at a fast food restaurant, Ronnie attends family child care. Sonia is an avid reader and stops often at the public library on her way home from work to get books for both herself and her son. A librarian has shown her the collection of board books in the children's room and has also suggested that she look at some simple nursery rhymes. Sonia shares these rhymes and other simple stories with Ronnie on the bus home, as she prepares dinner, and while Ronnie splashes in the bathtub. These home experiences are reflected in his deep interest in having stories told and read to him at child care.

Even at this early age, children's experiences at home have a powerful influence on their attitudes toward stories. It is also true that children's particular interests can affect the behavior of their families. Lucia's family loves to see her pleasure in music and encourages her by singing and dancing with her. Sonia is amazed to see Ronnie's deep interest in books and looks forward to sharing stories with him every day after work. Ronnie's and Lucia's obvious enthusiasm shapes their families' responses, which in turn help shape the children's interests.

Children's experiences at home have a powerful influence on their attitudes toward stories.

Development and the individual child

When we consider children's development, we need to keep in mind that some children will be ahead of what is considered "typical" and others will be behind, yet all are entitled to enjoy the story experiences discussed in this book. When working with children, especially those with special needs, we need to adapt the experiences we provide to reflect their responses. Though the focus of this book is on children age 3 and under, caregivers may find much of the information applicable to older children with special needs. (Chapter 5 has more specific information about sharing stories with children who have special needs.)

Clearly, many infants and toddlers will not fall exactly where charts or textbooks suggest they should in all areas of development. Some children will be *both* "ahead" and "behind," such as this 9-month-old:

> Mia is advanced in her language development and is just beginning to say words that can be identified by her parents and caregivers—words like *mama*, *no*, and *go*. She also likes to sit and look intently at picture books. But Mia has been slow to crawl and is still likely to stay where her parents or caregivers put her, seldom moving around to look for something new to examine.

Mia is using words earlier than most of her peers, and while she is not as physically active or advanced as many of the other infants in her child care program, she can attend to something she enjoys, such as pictures in a book, for longer than her age might suggest.

Discussion Starter

Eighteen-month-old Emma loves pictures of things with wheels and will sit quietly turning pages of her truck and car books for 15-minute periods during the day.

At age 2½, Ben likes variety in his stories, but his current favorite is one his caregiver tells often about a mother cat and her kittens and the adventures they have on the farm.

"Monster story!" begs 3-year-old Maria, bouncing up and down in anticipation, while David, 30 months, covers his ears and moans, "No monsters for Davey."

Imagine that you are the caregiver for the children in these three examples. How will you respond to each child in a way that respects that child's individual differences?

From Lullabies to Literature

A developmental continuum

Many books on child development describe in a comprehensive way what infants and toddlers typically know and can do at various ages and stages of development. Because of the great diversity across groups and among individual children, any developmental continuum has limitations. Nevertheless, such a resource can help us better understand very young children, as long as it is not seen as prescriptive.

For this book in particular, the continuum provided in Appendix A focuses on sharing stories by highlighting milestones that have implications for infants' and toddlers' enjoyment of stories and what adults can do to enhance this enjoyment. The chart links the various milestones with implications for sharing stories in ways that match and support development. These are only a selection from many possibilities; more are suggested throughout this book.

Understanding infant/toddler development and knowing what might be expected of children at different ages and stages—whatever scheme we choose to describe it—is essential knowledge for caregivers. Understanding how the children's development is supported and valued within their family and community contexts is just as important.

As children grow, learn, and develop, the story experiences they are involved in should become more complex. But the hallmarks of a quality story experience remain the same:

- Allowing unhurried time for conversations, sharing stories, and exploring pictures or books together.
- Being expressive and enthusiastic when sharing all types of stories.
- Following children's lead or interest in deciding what story experiences to provide and when to share a story.
- Sharing stories as part of everyday experiences.
- Supporting very young children's emerging skills and interest as story participants and storytellers.

With these hallmarks of good practice in mind, the following chapters move on to examine various story experiences and approaches in-depth. The next chapter considers spoken language—conversations, simple told stories, and language games.

Meow, said the cat . . . . Arf, arf, said the dog . . . . Oink, oink, said the pig . . . . Eee, eee, said

...onkey ... and the spider said nothing at all!

Sharing Spoken Language
Sounds, Conversations, Told Stories, and Language Games

The best teachers are the best storytellers.
—Frank Smith, *Exchange Every Day*

This chapter focuses on the spoken story experiences that infants and toddlers encounter early in their lives: conversations, oral stories, and language games such as songs and rhymes. Many adults are even surprised to learn that children this young need these kinds of natural language experiences at all. They may think, why would responding to an infant's gurgles or talking to a toddler about changing his diaper be important? After all, children this young do not talk much, if at all, and they can't understand everything adults say. Why shouldn't attention to language wait until later, when children can have "real" conversations?

In fact, there are direct links between young children being immersed in a range of different language experiences and their language development. Adults don't always recognize "language experiences" as such or understand their importance for very young children, but infants and toddlers are learning all the time from the stories, jokes, songs, and other spoken language they encounter in their particular culture, their family tradition, and the media (Dyson 1994). For example:

> Zia, at 8 months old, listens with her parents when they watch the news on television; Dean, age 2, listens to popular music on the

radio when he is in the car with his mom. Zia and Dean do not understand the words of the news or the songs, but they are learning how to tune into different sounds and that these sounds mean something.

We help very young children take a step along the path toward loving stories and becoming competent language users and storytellers when we provide experiences that foster enjoyment and engagement with sounds, symbols, and words, which are the precursors of the more complex structures we call stories. The more natural conversations and other spoken language experiences that infants and toddlers have in their very early years, the more likely they will become confident speakers, storytellers, and readers and writers when they are older (Schickedanz 1999; Rochat 2004).

To be very young children's "best storytellers," we need to:

- provide models of language in use;
- tailor experiences to respond to children's interests, needs, and backgrounds;
- encourage children to observe, listen, and imitate what they see and hear; and
- respond to and encourage infants' and toddlers' particular ways of communicating and storytelling.

This chapter describes spoken language experiences of all kinds. Most of the practical suggestions are suitable for English language learners and young children with special needs, provided that appropriate adaptations—such as using simple sign language to support language games—are incorporated. Many will be useful for older children with special needs, too. Focusing on what a young child *can* do as a communicator (rather than what she or he *cannot* do) and expecting that *every* child can be and become a good communicator are two principles that should underpin all our work with young children.

Beginning with sounds

How do we help very young children enjoy and engage with language and stories when they can't yet understand all of what we say? We start at the beginning—that is, with young infants and the sounds they make, imitate, and respond to.

Through daily exposure to human and environmental sounds, infants gradually become aware of how sounds are made and how they vary. This

> Infants gradually become aware of how sounds are made and how they vary.

From Lullabies to Literature

awareness is a necessary precursor to hearing and making the different sounds of the alphabet. Adults naturally and informally support infants' engagement with sounds and spoken language when they:

- draw children's attention to human and environmental sounds;
- model listening to these different sounds;
- point out the different qualities of sounds (e.g., loud and soft, high and low);
- move to sounds and music with children to help them hear and—particularly important for children with hearing impairments—"feel" different sounds through vibrations or motion;
- use language that rhymes; and
- vocalize with infants in response to their vocalizations.

Infants with special needs may require some different or additional experiences. An early intervention specialist can help infants develop their communication skills and can provide useful communication strategies for the caregiver. For example, a caregiver working with an infant with visual or hearing impairments might learn about combining simple sign language and physical actions with spoken words.

> Six-month-old Lakeisha has a visual impairment. Mandy, her caregiver, has learned to use touch as well as words to assist Lakeisha's understanding of spoken language. When Mandy says, "Now it's time to sleep in your crib," she gently places Lakeisha's hands on the side of the crib while emphasizing the word *crib*. Mandy repeats this tactile experience every day. Despite her difficulty seeing it, Lakeisha will gradually learn that a *crib* is where she is placed so that she can sleep.

> Ari is 10 months old and has a moderate hearing loss. One day, when he is sitting on the floor playing a toy drum with his hand, his caregiver Bella smiles at him and says, "Yes, Ari, you can make the drum go bang, bang, bang!" She takes his other hand and helps him feel the drum's vibrations as she bangs the drum with him. Feeling the vibrations can help Ari understand that there are sounds all around him and that he also can produce sounds with his actions.

Engaging in "conversations"

As discussed in Chapter 2, infants try to get their messages across (and they often succeed) even though their verbal language skills are not well developed. For example, a 3-month-old might cry to express her fright every time she hears the vacuum cleaner, but smile and coo to show her pleasure when her mother picks her up and sings songs to her.

Caregivers working with infants need to be skilled observers, learning to recognize each child's particular ways of communicating. Infants may communicate through crying, smiling, making noises, moving their hands and bodies—whatever they can do to convey their thoughts and feelings. When we respond to these sounds, gestures, and expressions, we engage infants in the early stages of a conversation. For example, an infant makes a happy gurgling noise, and his caregiver responds, "I can hear that you are a happy boy today!" Through interactions like this, the child is learning: "I make sounds, and the other person makes sounds back to me." In other words, he is learning the basic structure of turn taking in a conversation. These mutually enjoyable early conversations reflect the social nature of infants' learning and development (Rogoff 2003).

As infants grow into toddlers, they become more skilled at gaining and maintaining the attention of adults and other children by using a wider range of communication strategies. Sounds and gestures continue, but there is also an increasing use of vocalization, which is not always easy for adults to understand. However, it is critical that we try our best to show that we are making every effort to understand. That is one of the themes of *Knuffle Bunny*, by Mo Willems:

> Toddler Trixie's favorite stuffed toy is left behind at the Laundromat. Trixie tries to tell her father what has happened; she uses lots of made-up words and finally has a tantrum to express her feelings about the loss of her toy. Toddlers listening to this story might recognize Trixie's sense of frustration as she searches for a way to get her message across. Try as he might, Trixie's father does not understand her. Fortunately, Trixie's mother is quick to ask about Knuffle Bunny when an equally distressed father and child arrive home. The family rushes back to the Laundomat, and the father performs a heroic rescue by finding Knuffle Bunny in one of the washing machines.

Listening carefully and letting toddlers know when we understand what they are saying gives them the confidence and incentive to keep trying to use words and, eventually, sentences (Zambo & Hansen 2007). Some helpful practices in fostering toddlers' oral language development include:

• getting down to the toddler's level and making eye contact to show that you are listening;

• giving toddlers sufficient time and your full attention to help them get their message across comfortably;

- saying the correct form of the words and providing a simple elaboration as you respond to the toddler's comment; for example:

  "Dat ted … dat ted … me, me, me!"

  "Yes, Michael, that is your teddy, and you want it back."

- using simple signs taken from specific sign languages or representative gestures made up by adults familiar to toddlers who have communication difficulties; and
- using some simple, common words (e.g., *bottle*, *drink*, *yes*, *mom*) in the child's home language, if it is different from what is primarily spoken in the program.

These practices also reinforce warm and close relationships between child and adult, and they demonstrate our respect and genuine interest. From infants' early interest in and responses to sounds, to toddlers' increasing ability to convey messages through gestures, vocalizations, words, and sentences, we are nurturing this idea of having a conversation with someone.

Everything is new and fresh to young children, and adults will discover endless possibilities of talking about everyday activities with them. We might begin a conversation by naming objects: "That's your hat," "Here's your bottle," "There's teddy!" As children's listening vocabularies grow, we can use more complex comments and questions: "Let's watch the rain water our flowers," "Do you hear the dog barking?" "What do you think would be good for lunch today? Hot soup might be nice." Using a book is another way to support a conversation with an infant too young to converse with words, which New Zealand author Dorothy Butler (1998) has written about, and which will come up again in Chapter 5.

These exchanges are important not only because they familiarize young children with the conventions of conversation, but also because they help to tune infants and young toddlers into the beauty of language and how it supports and reflects our actions and experiences. These first narrations are important precursors to what are traditionally labeled as "stories."

Told stories

Sharing stories skillfully and enthusiastically is one of the best gifts we can give young children, and they will respond to our story gifts with interest, enthusiasm, and imitation, which are great rewards for caring adults. Sometimes our stories might reflect real events; other times we can allow our imaginations to soar in wild and wonderful ways. As infants become toddlers, the informal, simple stories we tell them can be extended and become more complex, with a deliberate plotline including a more elaborate group of characters, a distinct setting, and a set of events or a problem to solve.

Here are some types of simple told stories:

Real-life—We can tell about something the children are doing or something they might be interested in. For example, a story about a visit to a farm could be personalized by including children's names and the things they encounter there. Toy farm animals could be used to support the story.

Imaginative—Children are ready to be told stories of fantasy and "pretend" when they begin telling imaginative stories on their own. If several toddlers often sit in the dramatic play corner of the classroom and tell imaginative stories to the dolls or teddies there, they are probably ready for their caregiver to tell *them* similar stories.

Picture book—Picture book stories can be read just as they are written in a book, or we can adapt them in some way. For example, many adults know all the words in Eric Carle's picture book *The Very Hungry Caterpillar*. A caregiver could tell this story without using the book, sharing finger puppets with children instead of illustrations. Or the caterpillar in the story could be replaced by a very hungry puppy or other animal of interest to the children.

Folk tales—For very young children, folk tales may be better told and modified than shared directly from a book, as many versions are too scary for toddlers. Telling our own version allows us to make the story more age appropriate, and using large flannel figures or other props can make the story more inviting. For example, a modified telling of The Three Little Pigs could have all the pigs and the wolf working together to build a strong house, or The Gingerbread Man could be retold as a game of tag, where he invites animals and people to try to catch him as he runs all the way across the countryside to his home.

When stories relate to children themselves, they can be especially useful, as in this example:

> Jose works with older toddlers, and he likes to integrate informal stories naturally into everyday experiences. One day he observes Katie and Jackson "feeding" their dolls using pretend bottles. When he sees that they are both sitting and cuddling the dolls on their laps, he sits down and tells them a simple story.
>
> "One day, Katie and Jackson looked after the baby dolls in the Home corner. First they picked up the baby dolls, and then they

gave them bottles because the baby dolls were hungry. After they had given the dolls their bottles, Katie and Jackson cuddled their dolls and put them to sleep in their cribs."

Jose tells a story instead of simply commenting on what the children are doing. If he had chosen to comment, he might have said something such as, "I like the way you are caring for your baby dolls," or "Are your dolls going to sleep now?" But Jose decides to tell a story on this occasion because the children are sitting quietly and appear to be in the right mood for a story after their active play with the dolls. Hearing stories about their play enriches children's experience by affirming that play.

Listening to stories can evoke strong feelings in young children, helping them form deep connections with the storyteller and the characters. Hearing stories also helps children to learn, over time, the different ways stories are structured, their purposes, and the intonation patterns of the language. Eventually children begin to use similar structures in the stories they tell and later write.

Stories as connection

While infants and toddlers may not understand fully what the stories we tell them are about, they do listen and will gradually gain some understanding of why and how stories are told. Oral stories enrich young children's lives by helping to build connections with family members and community events. Children's memories of family and community life begin when they listen to and then actively participate in the sharing of stories. For example, children often ask their grandparents for stories about when their parents were very young. Sometimes these stories might be told when looking at family photographs; other times they are told as anecdotes.

Young children enjoy hearing stories like these over and over again, and it's not surprising: They are a way to connect young children with their family history and support the development of children's own identities within the family or child care program. Listening to and telling stories about our families or ourselves can be our way of telling others who we are or who we would like to be. Family child care homes and child care centers are also places rich in story potential about everyday events, the people who live in them, and their interests.

Told stories have to connect with the listener in the same ways as stories read from a book do. Through told stories, infants and toddlers start to learn that there is a connection among feelings, thoughts, and experiences

> **Listening to stories can evoke strong feelings in young children, helping them form deep connections.**

(Milne 2005). They learn that stories can arouse feelings and that the listener has to think about these feelings to comprehend the meaning of the story. This understanding—which infants and toddlers acquire across repeated story experiences—is necessary for children to later become competent readers and writers.

Oral storytelling traditions

Storytelling provides a way for us all to share our past experiences, present interests, and our future dreams. Stories help build relationships and share knowledge within a community (Magee & Jones 2004).

Long before books were widely available, and even before print was invented, people in communities all over the world told stories, which they passed down through generations of families. This tradition of telling stories continues today in many communities.

Examples of oral traditions can be found among Indigenous or First Nations peoples in the United States, Canada, Australia, and New Zealand. Many other countries have strong cultural connections across generations that are kept alive through the art of storytelling. Among other things, oral storytelling can:

• convey important beliefs and practices;

• remind children and adults of their responsibilities as members of a family, community, tribe, or kinship group;

• celebrate significant events or achievements;

• connect different generations to each other;

• provide entertainment; and

• explain natural phenomena, such as the wind or sunrise and sunset.

Storytellers in family groups or communities with a strong oral tradition are especially respected and valued for their contributions to society. Time for oral storytelling is set aside on a regular basis, as it is regarded as a priority.

How these oral stories are told, who tells them, the structure they follow, the focus of the content, and the purpose of their telling are different across cultural or kinship groups. Today, infants and toddlers all over the world listen to and learn from the told stories and oral traditions of their families and communities (Curenton 2006).

In societies where the oral tradition of storytelling is no longer central, stories still are a part of everyday life. Our interest in soap operas or reality television shows and the hours we sit while a friend tells us about something that happened recently are all connected with our deep enjoyment of and need for stories.

From Lullabies to Literature

Language play, rhymes, and games

Some of the simplest stories we tell very young children use language play, and they also flow naturally from our conversations with infants. It can be hard to carry on a conversation with a person who, however responsive and delightful, does not yet use words to talk back to us. As caregivers, we learn quickly that we may need to explore more creative ways to communicate to sustain both our own and the infant's interest in the conversation. For very young children, spoken language experiences can be extended through face or body games and rhymes. Though infants still will not understand many or even most of the words used, they will nevertheless enjoy the sound, rhythm, and tone of the language and the other creative elements of the experience. For older children, even if the words of a rhyme or finger game do not make sense, they still encourage children to explore and play with language. They also provide the raw materials for stories.

Face and body games are especially useful for nurturing relationships when they incorporate the sense of touch. Story games and language play might involve stroking or patting parts of the child's body, such as the hands, feet, knees, or head. These games require nothing more than a sensitive and knowledgeable adult and a relaxed infant.

Face and body games

With face games, a caregiver gently touches an infant's face while singing a song or reciting a rhyme or poem. For example:

> Kelly captures 3-month-old Gabe's attention as she sits beside him
> on the floor and recites:
>
> > Round and round the garden
> > Goes the teddy bear
> > One step, two step
> > Tickle him under there.
>
> As she speaks, she gently strokes around Gabe's face, finishing with
> a small tickle under his chin. Another time, Kelly knocks very softly
> on Gabe's forehead, saying:
>
> > Knock at the door
> > Peek in [touches Gabe's eyelids]
> > Lift up the latch ["lifts" his nose]
> > Walk in [points to his mouth]
> > Have a cup of tea
> > Under baby's chin! [tickles him lightly under the chin]

Some simple games extend beyond the face to other parts of the child's body. For example:

> When reciting "Hickory Dickory Dock," Kelly trails gentle fingers up Gabe's body to the top of his head; when she reaches the point in the story where the mouse runs down the clock, she runs her fingers quickly back down.

Games such as these offer interesting early story experiences for infants because they are short, rhythmic, rhyming, engaging, and have an element of suspense. They maintain the infant's attention and help foster a close relationship with the adult through the combination of words and touch.

While these games are used mostly with infants, toddlers will continue to enjoy them and will sometimes want to perform the actions in return on the adult. Toddlers will also play these language games with other children or with a toy. When toddlers start to recite the stories and perform the actions

Problematic language in nursery rhymes

By today's standards, many traditional Mother Goose–type nursery rhymes can seem violent, racist, sexist, or ageist. The Old Woman Who Lived in a Shoe is far from a loving mother, and Old Mother Hubbard has only a bone for her starving dog. In fact, traditional poems and songs in many cultures have elements that are of questionable appropriateness for young children.

Even though infants and toddlers will not understand many of the words or fully comprehend the messages, caregivers and families may still want to discuss which rhymes to share.

It seems unnecessary and unwise to reject all nursery rhymes on the basis of a few, especially if verses can be altered slightly to make the words, theme, or message more acceptable. "Three Blind Mice," for example, could be modified by changing the word *blind* to *kind*, and the farmer's wife can "cut them some cake with the carving knife" instead of cutting off their tales. It's an issue worth discussing among child care staff and with families.

with toys or with other children, it is a sign of their language learning: They are comprehending, remembering, and retelling language that they have heard and that they consider important.

The advantages for adults in using face and body games with young children are that nursery rhymes are short, easy to learn, and fun to share, even for those who may not have experience with them from their own childhood.

Lap games

Around the time children can sit up without support, they are ready to play lap games. The child sits on the caregiver's lap or ankles (for the latter, the adult sits in a chair with her ankles crossed, and the child sits securely on the adult's crossed ankles). The adult recites an appropriate rhyme, bouncing the child gently in rhythm with the words, adjusting the vigor of the bounce according to the child's reactions and the words of the rhyme. Here's one traditional British rhyme:

> *Ride a cock horse to Banbury Cross*
> *To see a fine lady upon a white horse.*
> *With rings on her fingers and bells on her toes,*
> *She shall have music wherever she goes!*

Another lap game is:

> *This is the way the lady rides—Jig, jig, jig*
> *This is the way the gentleman rides—Trot, trot, trot*
> *This is the way the farmer rides—Wobbly gee, wobbly gee*
> *And this is the way [child's name] rides!—Gallop, gallop, gallop*

In some versions of this lap game, the adult parts her knees slightly when it comes time for the child to "gallop," dipping the child carefully toward the floor.

More complex language play

As infants become toddlers, they are ready to engage in more elaborate forms of language play. For example, young toddlers are able to enjoy games that involve rapping on the table, dancing, singing, holding hands in a circle while marching, and finger movement games. Learning to open and close their hands to the accompaniment of "Open! Shut them . . . open! Shut them . . . give a little clap!" can be an exciting challenge, requiring them to control their fingers while responding to words rhythmically.

Finger games can become increasingly intricate as children's motor skills develop, although there are wide variations in how well toddlers are able to follow directions. For example, mastering the "proper" finger movements for

Family games and rhymes

Caregivers can encourage families to suggest songs and language games that can be shared with children in the program. These can be from a family's culture, country of origin, or home language.

This not only strengthens links between adults and children, but sharing games and rhymes remembered from childhood also creates bonds between adults, providing an opportunity for caregivers to discuss with families the importance of language while demonstrating respect for cultural traditions.

"Itsy Bitsy Spider" can be difficult for young children (and sometimes even adults!). Fortunately, complete accuracy is not what matters most.

Songs

Infants and toddlers are admiring and enthusiastic audiences for singers and songs of all kinds. Luckily for those of us with very little singing ability, children can be as captivated when we are singing off key and making up the words as we go as they are by the best mezzo-soprano. As with language games, singing and music combine well with physical activity. Most of us know that holding an infant while singing and dancing is one of the best ways to comfort the fussy child or to foster interest in place of boredom. Being sung to is an intimate language experience, which, when done regularly, can enhance an infant's enjoyment of language and strengthen the attachment between child and caregiver.

Songs with words are often stories set to music. Sharing them is an excellent way to introduce children to the ways words fit together, to melodies and rhythms, and to the unique sounds of their own and other languages. Infants and toddlers will move their bodies in response to music, waving their arms or clapping. Older toddlers also enjoy learning the words of their favorite songs, which enriches and increases their growing vocabularies.

Music experiences can be a wonderful addition to a child care program because they can help young children learn to listen carefully and selectively, a critical skill for enjoying and learning from stories. A well-chosen variety

Evaluating environmental sounds

We need to evaluate both the quality and quantity of sounds in our programs. We should ask ourselves: Is the environment noisy? Are there moments of peace and quiet? What are the prevailing sounds?

If the general noise level is too high, children will not adequately be able to hear and attend to conversations and stories. Concentration can be difficult when there are too many competing noises.

Moments of peace and quiet are important for children in care settings: Relative silence encourages conversation, creative use of language, and serious listening; and it helps children relax and feel comfortable. Very young children need to hear language clearly and require an environment that allows them to practice their emerging communication skills.

of music also helps children become familiar with the rhythms and sounds of their own and other cultures. However, this does not mean that music should be played so much that it turns into background noise. One concern often expressed about child care is that children are constantly stimulated by sounds. Even the best programs are noisier than a typical home.

Some children rarely experience silence or get opportunities to hear the sounds that occur naturally in their environments. *The Noisy Book*, a classic picture book by Margaret Wise Brown, wonderfully illustrates how interesting "silence" can be:

> When a little dog named Muffin has his eyes bandaged as a result of an injury, Muffin begins to hear all the interesting noises of silence: a clock ticking, a radiator gurgling, even the sound of his own tummy rumbling.

Very young children need opportunities to hear these kinds of sounds. We don't need to—and, in fact, we shouldn't—always rush to fill silences with conversation or music.

Discussion Starter

Think about rhymes, games, and songs you know that combine physical activity with language. Ask the families of children in your care, or other staff, to teach you verses they know and use in combination with physical actions.

1. How will you discuss the importance of these with staff and families?
2. How could you share these language games or rhymes with families?
3. How could you document the children's responses to these games?
4. Would written notes, photographs, audio or video tapes be the most helpful? Why?

Supporting toddlers as storytellers

Toddlers begin to tell their own stories when they can construct simple sentences, often around 2 years of age (Schickedanz 1999). For example:

> Anjali, age 2½, demonstrates the skills of a storyteller as she composes and sings a song while splashing in the bathtub at home:
>
> > Splash! Splash! Splash! [she slaps her hand onto the water]
> > Smash! Smash! Smash! [she squashes the sponge]
> > Anjali takes a bath
> > And sings.

A child's ability to create an original story does not necessarily mean that she has extraordinary talents. Most toddlers have the capacity to be creative with language, but their creative efforts must be encouraged by their families and caregivers.

As toddlers become more engaged with the stories we tell them, and as their facility with language develops, they begin to tell their own stories to toys, themselves, other children, and adults. We can document these stories by writing them down or recording them. These audio recordings and notes can be shared later with the child to stimulate further storytelling or to revisit a topic important to the child (see Chapter 7 for more on documenting storytelling and story participation). The documentation of these early story efforts can also be shared with families, who will see that their child's growing language competence is being recognized and encouraged.

Discussion Starter

1. What do you think adults can do to foster a child's pleasure and competence in language?
2. What kinds of story experiences might encourage a child to become a storyteller himself?

Toddlers often begin telling very simple stories as they are playing with objects, such as a doll or a toy truck. These stories can reflect their life experiences at home or in a program, as in the following examples of 2-year-olds:

> Ben, whose father drives a truck, pushes a big toy truck across the mat and says, "Daddy goed in truck . . . Brrrr, brrrr, brrrr."

> Mishca has often been rocked to sleep by her mother. One day in her program, she hugs a doll in the home corner and says, "Go to sleep, baby, go to sleep, baby."

> Ava, who lives on a farm, picks up a soft toy horse and pretends that it is running as she says, "Horsey run, my daddy's horsey runs here."

Caregivers need to listen closely to toddlers as they play so that we can acknowledge and encourage them to extend these first attempts at storytelling. We can do this with our questions and comments:

> "Where did your daddy go in his big truck today, Ben?"

> "Is your baby very sleepy, Mishca? Where will you put her to sleep?"

"Ava, can you make the horse run fast? Faster and faster the horse goes, over the hill and back home again."

By responding to their stories this way, we are sending children the message that we understand and value what they think and say. We can also use our comments to model grammatically correct language (such as *go* instead of *goed*) and some ways in which stories can be expanded with more information. For example:

"Ben, where will Daddy put his truck when he gets home?"

"Mishca, what will you do when your baby wakes up?"

"Ava, what would the horse like to eat when he comes back from his run?"

As children show that they understand what stories are, and as they begin to tell stories themselves, we may want to introduce the concept of "let's pretend" as a way of prompting or extending the child's developing storytelling. For example, at this stage a caregiver might tell a toddler, "Let's pretend that a tiny, tiny creature lives under this cubby, and let's make up a story about him. What do you think he'd like to have for lunch?" (Just be very careful that toddlers are ready for fantasy. Some may be unsure of how to react or fearful if they cannot yet understand the difference between real and imaginary.)

Vivian Paley's (2001) work with young children in the United States has shown that young children's competence as storytellers and listeners should not be underestimated. Children express themselves in a variety of styles as they try to understand their experiences, ask and answer questions, make predictions about what will happen next, and exercise their imaginations by creating stories of their own (Bardige & Segal 2005). In the next chapter, the focus shifts to the use of books as tools for enhancing language.

You want me to read this one? . . . You picked the book with the big, *truck. . . . The title of this book is Go!*

4

The Special Role of Books
Building a Story Collection to Share

Books are no substitute for living, but they can add immeasurably to its richness. When life is absorbing, books can enhance our sense of its significance.
—May Hill Arbuthnot, *Children and Books*

Books are particularly important story tools for introducing children to the power, pleasure, rhythm, and richness of language in print and pictures. We can use them to read a story aloud directly from the text, or to inspire an original story of our own, prompted by imaginative illustrations. Books are not just one among the many resources we might use in programs for very young children. Books warrant a special place in every program, center, and home. This chapter examines why that is, then offers guidance for putting together a collection of books appropriate for children age 3 and under.

Why books are special

Rare is the early childhood program without at least a few books among its toys and other materials. But the idea of incorporating books as an intentional and frequent part of a program for infants and toddlers specifically is relatively new. Like their reaction to language experiences for children of that age, many adults—caregivers and family members alike—are surprised, even skeptical, about the value of book experiences for children too young to read. Why exactly are books so important for them?

If you observe infants' and toddlers' interactions with books, you will have no doubt that they enjoy the experience—though *how* they show it might be very different from how adults would! Though they may not yet have the verbal skills to describe or request a story, they will bring us a book they like, clearly eager for us to share it with them. Children may point to a page or make a sound of delight to show their satisfaction with a story. They might listen carefully as we talk about the pictures or read aloud, or they can make it difficult for us to continue as they vocalize their enthusiasm! They may lean forward to examine the pictures closely, pointing to what they think is particularly important. They may flap, chew on, or even throw a book in excitement. They often anticipate a familiar book's climax by showing increasing excitement. Their smiles, rapt gazes, waves, claps, grunts, squeals, and full body wriggles tell us that they are absorbed in—and benefiting from—the book experience.

Their pleasure is reason enough to share books with infants and toddlers. But what else do very young children gain from books? Chapter 1 outlined three broad benefits of using stories with infants and toddlers. The following discussion illustrates the links between books and these benefits.

Books can enrich children's lives

The opening quote by May Hill Arbuthnot, from the classic work *Children and Books*, expresses one of the chief benefits of books: They can enrich our lives by deepening and expanding our experiences. This deepening need not be complex to be significant. For example, as a toddler looks at the pages of the wordless picture book *Shopping*, by Helen Oxenbury, she can associate her past experience of going shopping with her mother and, with adult help, see how the story differs from or is similar to her own shopping trips.

In the book, the central character pushes a button for the elevator in his high-rise apartment building in the city. This may be a novel experience to a child from a small town, who may be so interested that she does not want to go further than this very first page. On the other hand, a child who lives in an apartment building may view this summoning of the elevator as an ordinary occurrence and be eager to move on to the next page to see what happens next.

Building background knowledge

As adults, we each carry a rich store of memories, experiences, and learning that helps us make sense of the things that happen in our lives. Very young children are just building this store of knowledge, and sharing books with them can help. Children can study a picture of something they may have encountered and wondered about or something they have not yet experienced but that is of interest to them. Books can also help children reflect on the experiences they have had, or as Arbuthnot put it, books can enhance the "significance" of life. For example:

> Roberta shows 20-month-old Tomas a picture of a blue car in a book, saying, "Look, Tomas! There's a picture of a blue car just like your daddy's! You came here today in your daddy's blue car." She takes a toy car from a shelf and pushes it on the floor next to Tomas. "See, Tomas, the car is moving just like when you and your daddy drive along the road together!"

In this example, Roberta chooses a picture from a book that she thinks will interest the toddler, encourages reflection by calling his attention to it in a way that reminds him of his past experiences in the car with his father, and enriches his knowledge by relating the discussion about the picture in the book to an object in the present. Another time, perhaps, she will show Tomas pictures in Watty Piper's *The Little Engine That Could*, pointing out that the train, too, is blue like his daddy's car, and that people can ride in trains the way he rides in the car.

Anticipating the future

Sharing books with children can help them anticipate and prepare for things that may happen in the future. For example, sharing Margaret Wild's *Seven More Sleeps*, in which a child anticipates an upcoming birthday party, can add to a toddler's own excitement of his approaching birthday and show him how birthdays might be celebrated. Pictures and illustrations are particularly useful in this regard. For example, a picture book with a very simple story about moving into a new home may give a young child whose family is about to move a clearer idea of what is likely to happen than would simply talking about it or telling a story without using any pictures.

Exploring ideas

Stories and pictures in books provide good starting points for discussions with verbal toddlers. As we share books with children, we ask questions like, "I wonder why he's running away?" "That ice cream looks yummy—what do you like to eat?" and "That baby bird is sleeping in a nest. We don't sleep in nests, do we? Where do we sleep?" The following vignette shows how one caregiver tailored her book sharing to meet an individual child's needs:

Ladora is a family child care provider and works with four children, ranging in age from 4 months to 3 years. Daniel, one of the toddlers in her care, has a father whose work requires him to travel away from home often. Ladora notices that Daniel is often very quiet when his father goes away, so she decides to share with him the book *Lots of Feelings,* by Shelley Rotner, hoping it will help him express his feelings.

The next time his father is traveling, Ladora sits Daniel on her lap and they start looking at the book and its vivid photographs of children showing their feelings. Daniel looks very intently at the page that shows a child crying, and Ladora reads, "Sometimes we feel sad." She lets Daniel look at this page for a while, and then she asks, "Daniel, do you feel sad when your daddy goes away?" Daniel nods his head and points at the photograph. Ladora hugs him closer and says, "Yes, I can see that you get sad, but when Daddy comes back, you are glad to see him and then you feel happy! Let's look for more pictures about how children can feel." Daniel looks at this book several times throughout the day and wants Ladora to share it again with him the following day.

However, not every book sharing experience needs to have a discussion attached to it or lots of questions for the child. Overdoing questioning can spoil the simple joy and fun of sharing books. Every book experience does not have to include a lesson or moral, although we would hope that every book shared with a child enriches his or her life in some way. Good books can, and sometimes should, stand on their own.

Learning and imagination

Children enjoy their favorite books over and over again. As discussed in Chapter 1, repetition of familiar themes helps children gain a sense of confidence and allows them to gently explore new ideas and more complicated stories. Very young children like predictability, and text enables the reader to share the book in exactly the same way time after time (although sometimes children will urge us to vary the reading). This can be satisfying and reassuring to young children, who may sometimes find life surprising and unpredictable.

Books can enhance the present, provide escape, and tickle the imagination by helping children learn to envision something that is not currently part of their horizon. During the early months of life, infants cannot mentally maintain knowledge of an object that is outside their field of vision, but by the middle of the first year they seem to be able to recall (that is, imagine) an object that is out of sight. This capacity to know about an object that has

Very young children like predictability, and text enables the reader to share the book in exactly the same way time after time.

disappeared from view is a first step toward using imagination to envision people, places, animals, and events that young children have not directly experienced.

The ability to connect images and ideas to words that are spoken or read (that is, to imagine what the words mean) is especially important as children learn to interact with stories. To enjoy a fairy tale, for instance, a child must have a highly developed imagination. For very young children, imagining begins with simple images tied to real-life experiences, sometimes with a twist or change to make them interesting. For example, a caregiver might show an infant a picture of a dog and say, "There's a dog just like your dog, only this one has black spots and a long tail. Your dog has a brown coat and a short tail."

Books can strengthen relationships

Books offer models of the ways in which people love and care for each other. Many simple stories convey a sense of intimacy and affection, sometimes gently and seriously, as in *Goodnight Moon*, by Margaret Wise Brown, and *Full, Full, Full of Love*, by Trish Cooke; sometimes with a light touch that makes children chuckle, as in *The Napping House*, by Audrey Wood, a hilarious account of a family that piles people and animals on top of each other to take a nap.

Another important technique books employ to strengthen relationships is validating the worries of children, as in *Owl Babies*, by Martin Waddell, which follows three baby birds waiting for their mother to come home: When she does return, children are relieved to hear the message that "Mother's come back." Sharing a story such as this one lets children know that we understand their concerns and will help them to deal with their emotions.

Enjoying physical closeness

The act of sharing a book, whatever its contents, can strengthen relationships, as it almost inevitably means that adult and child are in close physical contact. In fact, one of the reasons for sharing books with no more than two or three children at a time is that it allows each child to nestle comfortably close to you, with opportunities to touch both you and the book, ask questions, and point to favorite pictures or characters (Neuman 2006).

Combining a relaxed physical closeness with a mutually enjoyed activity is important in building an affectionate relationship. Laughing together over the illustrated antics in *Silly Sally*, by Audrey Wood; clapping hands together like the babies in a picture; or chiming in on the words (or an approximation of them!) to *Chicka Chicka Boom Boom*, by Bill Martin, Jr.—these are mutually enjoyable activities that can be experienced in close physical contact, strengthening bonds of affection and trust between young children and their caregivers.

Books also can strengthen children's relationships with other children. A shared book experience gives toddlers something to talk about and build on in their play:

> After reading a story about mothers putting their babies to bed, 28-month-old Morag took her friend Seth by the hand, patted the rug next to her and indicated that she wanted him to lie down. Seth cuddled next to her and Morag patted his head gently and pulled a doll blanket up to his chin, just as she had seen the mothers in the book do.

Appreciating diversity

Books can also pave the way for understanding people in settings and communities different from the child's own. For example, the beautiful picture book *Mama, Do You Love Me?*, by Barbara Joosse, tells the story of an Inuit child testing the strength of her mother's love with the question, "Will you love me whatever I do and whoever I am?" Toddlers might notice that the child in the story lives somewhere different than they do, but the question is a universal one that they intuitively understand.

Illustrations also portray diversity. For example, Gwenyth Swains's book series for very young children focuses on children's everyday activities around the world, including *Wash Up, Carrying, Eating, Celebrating,* and *Bedtime*. The books have high-quality photographic images to capture the diversity of these experiences. Mem Fox's *Whoever You Are*, an excellent book to share with older toddlers, instead highlights the similarities among all children by pointing out feelings that all children have in common, regardless of background or culture.

Books can help children develop a sense of their own identity, which is crucial to forming relationships. Infants and toddlers are in the early critical stages of developing their sense of personal identity: Who am I? Am I a worthwhile person? Do I fit in? Am I lovable? (Puckett & Black 2007). How children feel about themselves is as important to their overall development as their learning is (Bardige & Segal 2005). As children develop a sense of personal efficacy, they become more confident about exploring, taking risks and trying things out. Adults who are supportive of a child's efforts contribute to that child's feeling of self-worth and let her know that others share

Books can help children develop a sense of their own identity.

many of the same feelings and challenges. Books can provide additional evidence that other people—those who are like them, but also those who are different in some ways—share the same emotions, have the same concerns, and face similar challenges.

Books can support emerging literacy

Children who have lots of experiences with books absorb the rhythms and patterns of language and, at surprisingly early ages, begin to imitate the language and gestures their caregiver uses while sharing stories, sometimes turning pages and murmuring as they "read" the pictures. While we can't expect infants and toddlers to be learning to read and write yet, they are nevertheless developing skills that provide a foundation for later literacy. Sharing books with very young children supports emerging literacy by:

• helping children learn that pictures and words are symbols that can be interpreted;

• exposing them to new words, thereby increasing their vocabularies; and

• familiarizing children with the conventions of print.

Understanding pictures and print as symbols

Within their first 18 months, most infants who have explored and shared books with adults show an understanding that pictures symbolize things in the real world, an understanding that is uniquely human (Barton & Brophy-Herb 2006). For example, at around 12 months, an infant seems to understand that the cup in a picture on the page represents a cup like the one she drinks from every day. She may indicate the connection she is making by looking at the picture and pointing to a nearby cup. Another child, age 17 months, enjoying the book *Goodnight Moon* with his dad, may murmur, "Hush," when his dad turns to the page about a quiet old lady who was whispering, "Hush" (Schickedanz 1999). Understanding that pictures are symbols of real things is a first step toward understanding that print also represents ideas of items in the real world.

Children may begin to notice print in addition to pictures between 15 and 20 months, and by 32 months a child may move a finger or her whole hand across a line of print and verbalize her memory of what the text says (Schickedanz 1999). Although we might find constantly answering the question, "What say?" exhausting, children's recognition that pictures and print convey meaning is an important step in emerging literacy that we need to support by responding to their inquiries (Neuman, Copple, & Bredekamp 2000).

Using *Knuffle Bunny*

A good example of a book that is beneficial to children in multiple ways is the delightful *Knuffle Bunny*, by Mo Willems (introduced in Chapter 3). This book tells the story of Trixie, a toddler whose favorite bunny gets left behind during a trip to the Laundromat. Sharing *Knuffle Bunny* can:

Enrich children's lives by affirming, valuing, and extending what they know about the world and themselves. Toddlers who accompany their parents to the Laundromat each week will relate to Trixie's experiences. For other toddlers who have never had that experience, sharing this story might extend what they already know about washing clothes while exposing them to a new concept—a trip to the Laundromat.

Strengthen relationships through the physical closeness and conversation that is intrinsic to sharing books with infants and toddlers. Toddlers who have a favorite toy may connect emotionally with Trixie, who loses and then finds her favorite stuffed animal at the Laundromat.

Support emerging literacy as infants and toddlers begin to learn how stories and books "work." *Knuffle Bunny* gives very young children the opportunity to learn about the structure of a story (that it has a beginning, middle, and end, as well as characters and a plot) and how print and pictures convey or tell the meaning of the story.

Increasing vocabulary

Sharing books will expand very young children's growing vocabularies. Storybooks often use words in ways that are different from how they are used in everyday conversation. Books also use words that are generally absent from day-to-day speech. *The Napping House*, for example, contains many descriptive words related to napping, such as *slumbering, snoozing*, and *dozing*, which may only rarely occur in a conversation between an adult and a child. By hearing new words in the context of a story and having them explained by an adult, children's word comprehension will grow, and they will eventually incorporate new words into their spoken vocabularies.

Learning the conventions of print

Through early exposure to books, children begin to learn about the conventions of reading in their own language. For example, very young children using books in English learn that they are read from front to back, from the left of the page to the right, and from the top of the page to the bottom. Books in some other languages have different print conventions. Children learn that books have names (or "titles") and that they are written by "authors." Some older toddlers might be interested in books whose layouts break the rules; for example, books that are read from back to front, from right to left, or up and down the page in vertical columns.

Discussion Starter

If a parent or colleague asks you why you would use books with infants and toddlers, how would you answer in your own words? Write down your possible responses.

Types of books

The variety and abundance of books can make selection both fun and challenging. The following overview of the types of books available will help as you start or expand your collection of books to use with infants and toddlers. The overview categorizes books in two overlapping ways: by *content* (i.e., subject matter, fact or fiction) and by *construction* (i.e., the particular materials used to make the book).

Content

Five broad types of books are described below, categorized by their content: (1) information and concept books; (2) books with story lines; (3) books that feature nursery rhymes, poems, or songs; (4) personal books; and (5) books not produced with very young children in mind but that nevertheless may interest this age group.

Information and concept books

Very young children have limited experience with the world in which they live. Books can help an adult describe or explain objects, animals, people, and phenomena that are of interest to children. For example, a picture book about animals can include pictures of animals with which the child is familiar, but can also introduce animals that are new to her. A book about cars and trucks can be informative and satisfying to a child who is interested in vehicles of all kinds.

Books don't always have to include a story to offer very young children the kind of learning experience they will find deeply interesting. Information books written for infants and toddlers might feature a simple picture of an object or animal on each page, often but not always accompanied by an identifying label or other brief text. Such books for very young children are often about everyday or common subjects such as farm animals, "things that go," families, food, toys, or household objects. The book *Animals*, by Roger Priddy, for example, contains photographs of animals accompanied by their names.

Alphabet and counting books are a particular type of information book. Very young children can enjoy them, but children should not be expected to memorize the alphabet or learn to count at this age:

> When Juan shares the book *So Many Bunnies,* by Rick Walton and Paige Miglio, with 2½-year-old Clara, he does not try to teach her the letters of the alphabet or how to count the number of bunnies on each page. He simply reads the rhyming text, occasionally running his finger under it as he reads, and allows Clara to enjoy the fun of an amusing tale that also happens to be an alphabet and counting book.

A concept book is about an abstract subject or theme, such as colors, shapes, or sizes. These books usually display a picture representing some dimension or variation of the concept on each page. Like information books, the picture is often accompanied by a label or a bit of explanatory text. A book about colors, for example, might have several red objects on a page with the word label "Red." Here are some good concept books:

- *What Color?*, by Anthea Sieveking, uses beautiful color photographs of objects and children.
- *Olivia's Opposites,* by Ian Falconer, uses the popular book character Olivia the Pig to teach young children the concept of "opposites."
- *Black on White* and *White on Black,* both by Tana Hoban, are wordless concept books that contain images of black everyday objects on white pages, and vice versa.

The knowledge children gain from information and concept books expands their understanding of the world, making them important precursors to and aids in understanding both told and read stories. Caregivers can share information and concept books just as they are, but we can also use them in creative ways as the subjects of or starting points for conversations and stories.

Discussion Starter

1. When do you use information or concept books?
2. How do the children you work with respond to these books?

Signing in books

Some recently published information and concept books include hand signs as well as text; that is, the text is accompanied by images of corresponding signs. Books that include pictured signs can also be immensely useful when working with a hearing impaired child; both adults and children can learn simple signs.

Some classic picture books such as *Brown Bear, Brown Bear, What Do You See?*, by Bill Martin, Jr., and *Goodnight Moon*, by Margaret Wise Brown, are available in sign language editions. Reputable bookshops and children's librarians will be able to locate and order them.

There are several sign languages; two commonly used English-based sign languages are American Sign Language (ASL) and Australian Sign Language (AUSLAN). It is not always possible to tell which sign language a book is presenting unless the person selecting the book is knowledgeable about signing. For hearing children who are learning signs to augment communication, the specific language may not matter, but for a hearing impaired infant it will be important to select books in the sign language the child and family will use.

Examples of books that use ASL include these:

• *My First Book of Sign Language*, by Joan Holub

• *Sign and Sing Along: Twinkle, Twinkle, Little Star*, by Annie Kubler

• *Meal Time*, by Anthony Lewis

Publisher Child's Play has produced a series of delightful books for babies and toddlers that use Australian Sign Language. These books include diversity in a natural way and provide clear instructions for adults about the appropriate signage to use while sharing the book.

Books with story lines

Storybooks appropriate for infants and toddlers usually have a central character or characters with whom the child can identify. These characters have adventures of the everyday sort, such as getting dressed, eating, and going to bed; or their adventures can be silly or wild, designed to amuse children and tickle their imaginations. Good examples of books with imaginative story lines that evoke familiar experiences include:

Beach Party!, by Harriet Ziefert, in which a variety of animals parade across the beach, each moving in a unique way. Toddlers will laugh at the idea of animals having a beach party and might like to pretend to move like the animals depicted in the book (sliding or twisting or scooting, for example).

Does a Kangaroo Have a Mother, Too?, by Eric Carle, in which the question repeats for many different animals, some of whom will be familiar to the children and others unfamiliar. The simple story line conveys the message that every animal and every human has a mother, and that all mothers love their children.

My Dad!, by Charles Fuge, in which Baby Bear boasts to his friends about his big, strong, rough, tough Daddy Bear, but when he finds himself alone in the jungle, it is Daddy Bear's warm cuddle that he wants most of all. Many toddlers would recognize the comfort of this type of cuddle.

Some books, such as Judy Hindley's *The Big Red Bus*, combine a simple story (about a bus ride) with information (about forms of transportation). This particular picture book appeals to children who are fascinated by things that move, such as buses and trucks. Children will enjoy participating in the adventures of the big red bus by calling out words such as *stop* and *help* at the appropriate moments in the story.

While many books for very young children that contain story lines use both words and pictures, others are wordless or have very few words. Even without text, the best of these books still convey character, time, and plot. They are wonderful resources, as the illustrations or photographs can spark the imagination and serve as jumping-off points for storytelling by adults *and* children. Excellent examples include *Changes, Changes*, by Pat Hutchins; *Color Farm*, by Lois Ehlert; the *Very First Books* series, by Helen Oxenbury; *The Red Book*, by Barbara Lehman; and *Picnic*, by Emily Arnold McCully.

Art-based books

The category of art-based books, though small, is worth mentioning because some children and their families find them particularly appealing. These books use the work of well-known artists as illustrations. One example is the book *A Magical Day with Matisse*, by Julie Merberg and Suzanne Bober, a board book that has a very loose story that corresponds with well-known paintings by the artist Henri Matisse. Art-based books can be found in specialty bookstores and museum shops.

Books featuring nursery rhymes, simple poems, or songs

This category overlaps with books with story lines, as nursery rhymes and some poems and songs usually tell a story. For example, in *Busy Toes*, C.W. Bowie uses rhyming text about toes, which offers toddlers the opportunity to enjoy wiggling their toes while they listen. *Hush Little Baby*, by Sylvia Long, is a wonderful example of a story told in a song. Some books featuring nursery rhymes, poems, and songs also have particularly well-done illustrations. The stories and the language in this category of books can be exciting, funny, soothing, relaxing—and almost always engaging for very young children.

Personal books

These are original books made from photos and drawings, clippings from brochures, magazines, greeting cards, and other documents and materials that tell a story about a child's personal experiences, such as a vacation or a group walk to the park. These are valuable additions to any collection. They are often favorites of young children, especially if they are introduced and shared by adults who are eager to talk about the pictures and their personal significance.

Other books and printed material

This category includes but is not limited to travel, nature, recipe, and art books, and even brochures, catalogues, and instruction manuals! We need to appreciate that occasionally children will show great interest in books and other printed materials not produced with them in mind.

Books intended for older children and adults may interest infants and toddlers particularly if there are clear, prominent pictures or diagrams and the subject draws the child in. When one caregiver took a field guide into her program to help a colleague identify a bird, one of the infants discovered the book and sat for periods of 20 minutes at a time over several days studying the pictures with rapt attention. Sometimes an infant or a toddler will be truly fascinated by a picture or diagram that reflects his or her own highly unique taste. For example:

> Toddler Rosie became fascinated with the diagram-filled instruction booklet that came with her family child care provider's new washing machine. She asked her caregiver to "read" it with her so often that the caregiver finally begged Rosie's father to *please* take it with him to share with Rosie at home.

Discussion Starter

1. What are some examples of "unorthodox" books or other materials that have been particularly enjoyed by the children with whom you work?
2. How did you discover that the children were interested in these materials?
3. How did you discuss these interesting selections with families?

Construction

A second way to categorize books for very young children is by the way they are made. This can include board books, Big Books, fabric and plastic books, as well as pop-up and novelty books.

Board books

Board books are some of the most commonly available for young children. They have heavy cardboard pages, which makes them appropriate for older infants and toddlers who may want to look at books on their own. These children are trying hard to use the books carefully and want to turn pages but have not mastered the art of enjoying books without damaging or tearing them. Some board books are fairly "chunky," maybe three and a half inches square by an inch or more thick. This is a convenient size for infants, who are mastering the use of their hands, as a book this small can be held comfortably; the pages are fat enough for infants to turn and sturdy enough to withstand their practicing. Toddlers like to carry them around, sharing and "reading" them to dolls and teddy bears along the way.

> **Sharing a book should be an intimate experience for infants and toddlers.**

    Board books are available in standard picture book sizes, as well. These are perhaps the most familiar and popular books in early childhood programs—they are sturdy and can withstand being flapped about, carried, and used as supplementary play materials. They are also big enough for a caregiver to share them with two or three children nestled closely by her side.

Big Books

A variety of picture books are available in oversized Big Book format. These books can be useful if one adult is responsible for presenting a book to a large group of children, for example. However, sharing a book with an adult and perhaps one or two other children should be an intimate experience for infants and toddlers. In this situation, Big Books can be unwieldy. It is difficult for the adult to turn pages with a lap full of small children or, if they are sitting next to her, to hold the book for each child to see the pictures as closely as children in this age group usually demand. It may work for a Big Book to be placed on the floor for one or two children to share with the adult. In general, however, for children under 3, Big Books are not the most appropriate choice.

Fabric books

Fabric books (similar to what used to be called "rag" books) are usually intended for very young infants. They are constructed to be flapped, chewed, squashed, and otherwise used roughly, then thrown in the washing machine. Beautiful handmade fabric books often can be found at craft markets or fairs in addition to more general bookstores. These books should be inspected carefully before being handed over to infants to be sure there are no safety hazards, such as buttons or loose parts that could be pulled off.

Plastic books

Plastic books (sometimes called "bath" books) are like fabric books in that they are made to withstand rough handling. But plastic books can be submerged in water or squashed without permanent damage. Of course, allowing them to be treated roughly can cause some confusion, as infants and toddlers may not grasp fully that paper books cannot take the same immersing and squashing! Plastic books also are easy to clean, which is an advantage, especially when they are used in a group situation.

Generally, however, plastic books are the least useful for book experiences, typically because they are created more for play purposes. For example, a bath book might position a small object, such as a teaspoon, on a page facing a large object, such as a tractor, but the objects are depicted as being the same size. Many plastic books have background scenes or borders in bright colors, making it hard to determine what is supposed to be the central object on the page. Finding high-quality plastic books requires time and patience.

Pop-up, lift-the-flap, and other novelty books

Novelty books for infants and toddlers typically offer a simple story or a collection of pictures plus a special physical feature, such as a flap that opens to reveal a picture underneath or a cutout so children can see through to the next page. *Peepo!*, by Janet and Allen Ahlberg, and *Whose Tail?* or *Whose House?*, by Jeanette Rowe, are good examples of these types of books. Jeanette Rowe's series of lift-the-flap books are suited to younger children because they have simple story lines with matching pictures in bold colors. Importantly, the flaps are half the page, which makes it easier for small hands or fingers to lift them.

Other novelty books may involve the child in an activity, such as feeling different textures on the page, hunting for hidden objects in the illustrations, fitting puppets or other objects into pockets in the illustrations, or clapping or jumping as prompted in the text. Books with objects or textures to touch are particularly helpful for infants and toddlers with visual impairments.

Discussion Starter

Think about the books you share with children.

1. What content categories do they represent? How are they made?
2. Is your collection of books balanced? That is, are there too many of a certain type and not enough of another?

Building a book collection

There are so many books from which we can choose. Evaluating and selecting books is challenging; for while it is true that practically any book is better than no book at all, providing the best and most appropriate materials is an important indicator of quality in an early childhood program. With that in mind, this section focuses on guidelines for putting together or adding to a collection of books for infants and toddlers.

Variety

The most important aspect of building or adding to a collection is ensuring variety. A range of books from the categories discussed above should be made available. Generally, younger children need just as much exposure to information and concept books as older children do because of their keen interest in the world around them. However, at a surprisingly young age, many children will become interested in simple stories and books with more complex content, as well. *Splash!*, by Flora McDonnell, has bold illustrations that support an interesting story that is suitable for very young children. Todd Parr has a series of books for young children with very brightly colored but simple illustrations. The series includes *The Peace Book*, *The Daddy Book*, *The Mommy Book*, and *The Family Book*; the simple text would provide a starting point for sharing a story with toddlers.

It is difficult to predict what will catch children's attention, and occasionally a book which seems to be "too old" for a child will become a personal favorite. Be sure to include in your collection a few books and other printed materials (such as catalogues) that were not written with this age group in mind. As discussed earlier, children sometimes find these resources quite fascinating.

Infants under 6 months of age, in particular, will enjoy the rhythm and fun of books that contain a nursery rhyme, short poem, or song accompanied by pictures. Books with textures to feel may also be attractive to infants.

They are captivated by the pictures of other babies, such as the big round faces so aptly portrayed by illustrator Helen Oxenbury in books such as *Clap Hands* and *Say Goodnight*. Photo albums of the child's family and pictures of the familiar experiences in the child care program, black-and-white designs in a picture book, and books with interesting pictures and a single word of text will be enjoyed by the youngest infants and in a different way by older children.

As infants grow older, they enjoy brief stories and pictures about animals, objects, and people, as well as special features such as lift-the-flaps and embedded noises. Although much is known about typical patterns of development (see Chapter 2), each child is unique. No two children of identical age will have exactly the same skills, understandings, or interests. Because of this rich individual variation, very young children's preferences for stories, books, and other printed materials range considerably. Consider the following example:

> In Terrence's toddler room, the 2-year-olds all enjoy different story experiences. Dominic likes listening to his caregiver recite nursery rhymes. He tries hard to imitate what he is hearing—something usually expected of older children. Freya likes picture books with fairly complicated plots and listens with close attention to stories intended for 3- and 4-year-olds. Samantha is more interested in simple board books with one or two words on each page. And some children in Terrence's room seek out both simple board books *and* more complicated stories.

Other factors

There are a number of qualities to consider, in addition to variety, when building a collection. Those related to content include:

- engaging text, if text is present, which adds to the overall impact of the story as it helps to keep children interested;
- familiar subjects;
- portrayal of inclusion and respect for diversity;
- absence of bias and stereotypes;
- emotions reflected and explored;
- appeal to a wide age range;
- humor and imagination;

- sensitivity to the culture, language, and values of families in the program; and

- appropriate use of fantasy elements.

Other qualities have to do with the overall presentation and format, including:

- excellent artwork;

- whether part of a series or a stand-alone;

- availability of accompanying narration (audio, video);

- sturdiness and safety for independent use and rough handling; and

- special qualities that adults can share with children.

Even though each book does not need to feature all of these qualities, the range of books in a collection should reflect all of them. Each of these elements is discussed below.

Engaging text

You won't always be reading books with text, and you may not always read those books that do have text word for word. Nevertheless, pay attention to the text as you choose books for your collection. Include some books that contain rhyming or repetitive text and that play with sounds in interesting ways. These books not only introduce children to the rhythm of spoken language, but they also increase vocabulary and lay the foundation for the development of phonemic awareness. Some good examples of books that use rhyme to foster children's interest in sounds and words are:

- Kevin Lewis's *Chugga-Chugga Choo-Choo*;

- Paul O. Zelinsky's *Knick-Knack Paddywhack*; and

- Bill Martin, Jr.'s *Brown Bear, Brown Bear, What Do You See?*; *Polar Bear, Polar Bear, What Do You Hear?*; and *Panda Bear, Panda Bear, What Do You See?*

Learning to read requires that children have considerable awareness of the sound structure of spoken language (Neuman, Copple, & Bredekamp 2000). Phonemic awareness—the ability to recognize and manipulate the smallest units of meaningful sound in a language or, more specifically, in words—is one of the skills most important in predicting reading success in the early school years, as it helps children hear similarities and differences in spoken words. This later translates into making the letter-sound connections necessary for understanding printed words (Juel 2006). While formal teaching or drill for infants and toddlers is unnecessary and inappropriate, learning to listen to and find fun in sounds and combinations of sounds (such as in "Baa, Baa, Black Sheep" or "Hickory Dickory Dock") can provide an important and joyful starting point for language play. Such play will lead to phonemic awareness and, eventually, to literacy.

Familiar subjects

Include many books that are about familiar objects, people, animals, or events in children's lives. The world is a new and unfamiliar place for the very young child. A picture of an everyday object "just like mine!" or a simple illustration of a young child doing familiar things can be both exciting and reassuring. The series including *Let's Go to Bed*, *Let's Feed the Ducks*, *Let's Have Fun*, by Pamela Venus, and the book *Eat Up, Gemma*, by Sarah Hayes, are examples of stories about everyday activities for very young children.

Portrayal of inclusion and respect for diversity

Choose books that reflect the lives and communities of the children in your program, but also include books that introduce children to other lifestyles and cultures. In other words, the books in your collection should reflect both cultural similarities and differences. Infants in particular love to see pictures of other children. This natural curiosity provides a great opportunity to introduce them to wide-ranging diversity in books. Add to your collection books with pictures of infants and toddlers in other communities, countries, and cultures, wearing different clothes, eating different foods, and being carried in different ways. For example, the book *Bread, Bread, Bread*, by Ann Morris, uses photographs to show different breads enjoyed by loving families and happy children around the world. Books like these also show that all over the world, children are cared for by people who love them.

Books can play an important role in helping children accept and respect diversity of many kinds. Between the ages of 2 and 3, children typically become more interested in the physical characteristics of others. They may ask questions or point out differences they notice, such as skin color or physical ability. Books by Helen Oxenbury (e.g., *Clap Hands*, *All Fall Down*, *Say Goodnight*) portray infants and toddlers of several ethnicities playing and having a good time together—certainly a gentle and appropriate way to introduce and acknowledge diversity with very young children. When we share books that have diversity embedded in them in a natural way, children are able to become familiar with differences among everyone and to understand that they are normal.

Author Vera B. Williams also takes this inclusive approach, featuring children of many backgrounds interacting with each other without calling attention to their differences. Her books *"More More More," Said the Baby* and

Between the ages of 2 and 3, children typically become more interested in the physical characteristics of others.

Music, Music for Everyone are good examples of unobtrusive diversity, as is *I Smell Honey*, by Andrea and Brian Pinkney. *Where's Chimpy*, by Berniece Rabe, focuses on the story while naturally incorporating a character who has additional needs. Other books that depict diversity, including disability, in a natural way, include Marjorie W. Pitzer's board book *I Can, Can You?* and *A Nice Walk in the Jungle*, by Nan Bodsworth, suitable for older toddlers. In *Mama Zooms*, by Jane Cowen-Fletcher, a child has many wonderful adventures with his mother. Gradually the illustrations reveal that the mother is in a wheelchair, but do so in a very matter-of-fact way. The emphasis of the story is on the relationship between mother and child and the fun they are having together.

Sometimes children who have special needs are excluded by their program from opportunities to play and participate in stories with their peers and are instead made to focus on skill development. But rich story experiences are important for *all* children in a group to enjoy and benefit from. Moreover, just like their peers, children with special needs should be able to see themselves in the books we share. For example, personal books that include photos of assistive devices such as special spoons, cups, and chairs can help the whole group appreciate the skills that children with special needs are developing and the tools that are needed to help them.

All these kinds of inclusive books help children to understand and appreciate one another's strengths and challenges, helping to build bonds of attachment between and among them. Children's librarians are wonderful resources for finding books about children from a variety of backgrounds, books for young children in other languages, and books about people with additional or special needs.

Absence of bias and stereotypes

Reject any book that depicts bias or stereotypes related to gender, culture, background, age, disability, and the like. Books can be powerful influences on a child's beliefs and values. From infancy, children begin to form attitudes toward others. Many old picture books are surprisingly sexist, as are some recent ones. Books should not feature only brave, active male people or animals, nor only quiet, demure female people or animals who never have adventures. Such stereotypes are not helpful to young children who are forming a gender identity. Be sure to share some books like *Dimity Dumpty: The Story of Humpty's Little Sister*, by Bob Graham. In this story, it is Humpty Dumpty's sister who saves the day when things go awry!

The bias in some books is blatant and obvious, and most of us would agree that these books are unsuitable. However, there are likely to be a number of books about which people will have varying opinions, and there is room for lively debate and discussion about what is appropriate and what is not in the early childhood setting. The good news for those selecting books is that we can afford to be critical and choosy, as there are so many excellent books available.

Emotions reflected and explored

Books that explore feelings—happiness, sadness, anger, fear, jealousy, worry—interest toddlers when they can relate to the depicted situations or emotions. One of the developmental tasks for very young children is to learn to identify their feelings and express them appropriately. Books such as *My Mum Goes to Work*, by Kes Gray, can help children learn to do this. This book has a simple text and illustrations and expresses the emotions a toddler might feel when his mother (or another family member) goes to work. Shelley Rotner's *Lots of Feelings*, mentioned earlier, features wonderful photographs of a diverse group of children showing their feelings.

Appeal to a wide age range

Choose books that are likely to appeal to a range of ages and remain interesting as children develop and gain more understanding of the world around them. Good books grow with children—that is, the books can make the transition from infancy, when many children simply look at illustrations, to toddlerhood, when children become more intrigued by the story line.

Also keep in mind that some children love short simple picture books but are not ready yet for more complicated stories, such as those in the *Frances* series, by Russell Hoban. Other children under the age of 3 may listen happily to these same stories and assert with disdain that simpler books are "for babies!"

Choose books that an adult can make interesting for infants and toddlers but can also interest children when they use them on their own. Pay attention to both text and illustrations. The classic picture book *The Very Hungry Caterpillar*, by Eric Carle, can make this transition, as its illustrations and text both are strong enough to interest children as they grow and develop. Infants and young toddlers may enjoy looking at the pictures in the board book version, while older toddlers can actively participate in sharing the traditional version. Eventually, through continued exposure to the same book, young children learn to "read" the text of a story by reciting the lines that have become familiar as they turn the pages.

Discussion Starter

Think about how you might share a book you are thinking of including in your collection with an 8-month-old, a 20-month-old, and a 3-year-old. Write down your thoughts and share them with others.

Humor and imagination

Choose books that will foster young children's active imagination and sense of humor. *Good Night, Gorilla*, by Peggy Rathmann, contains the type of humor that delights very young children. It is the story of a monkey who unlocks a zoo's cages after the zookeeper has said goodnight to the animals. Toddlers relish the illustrations of all the animals asleep in the zookeeper's bedroom in this wonderful picture book. *What Shall We Do with the Boo-Hoo Baby?*, by Cressida Cowell, is another book that infants and toddlers find amusing and will demand to have read again and again. Infants will enjoy the pictures in these books, though they may not understand the story.

Sometimes sharing a humorous, imaginative story does not unfold as we expect. Consider this brief sharing of *Silly Sally*:

> While sitting down one day to read with three toddlers in her program, Jennie has *Silly Sally* thrust upon her by 3-year-old Toby, who begins to giggle as Jennie opens the book. She reads the first page: "Silly Sally went to town, walking backwards, upside down," while Toby stands up and demonstrates how to walk backward. Giggling, the other two join him—and that is the joke and the story for the day.

Sometimes one page of a good book is enough!

Sensitivity to the culture, language, and values of families in the program

Effective communication with families will help us determine which books are appropriate for the children in our programs and which are not. It may be useful and enlightening for caregivers and families to talk about their opinions on including books that, for example, give human attributes to animals, discuss strong emotions (including negative ones!) candidly, or portray children as "naughty" or adults as unkind. Discussing topics such as these may help caregivers and families realize the extent to which the stories we choose reflect our cultural biases and values.

For example, the parent of a 3-year-old objected to the use of the picture book *The Grouchy Ladybug*, by Eric Carle. The ladybug in the story would like to have a friend but isn't very good at making one; she thinks she is bigger and better than everyone else, and she continually asks other creatures, "Want to fight?" At last she makes friends with another ladybug. The mother who objected to the book thought it gave the message that you can only be friends with people who look like you, and she disliked the repeated use of the question "Want to fight?"

Talking with families about the values, both positive and negative, that they find reflected in children's books can help guide your selection of books. When we select books with care and consider the needs of children and their families, we can support children in important ways:

> Bryn is concerned about 2-year-old Melissa, whose parents are planning to divorce. Bryn suggests that both parents might like to look at the picture book *Two Homes,* by Claire Masurel, to see if they might find it helpful to read with Melissa. They are delighted to share the book with Melissa, and Melissa's father is inspired to make a book for her out of photos of the two homes Melissa will soon have.

To support children and families, we also need to include in our collections books written in the first language of each of the families in the program. It can be interesting to all children to hear a familiar story in a language other than English, especially if the story is accompanied by detailed illustrations. Sharing a Spanish language version of a familiar story, such as *The Very Hungry Caterpillar*, demonstrates respect for Spanish-speaking children and families. At the same time, using this well-known book in a new way is a chance to talk about languages while engaging children who are already familiar with the story but do not speak Spanish.

Some simple books for toddlers feature a single picture of a different object on each page, such as a chair or a tree, labeled in both English and another language. Such books can help both caregivers and children learn a few words in the home languages of children in the program. Other books tell more elaborate stories, with the text presented side-by-side in English and in another language. Some examples of dual-language books are *Sleepyhead*, by Nicola Smee; *Bear in a Square*, by Stella Blackstone; and *Where Is Baby's Belly Button?*, by Karen Katz. Incorporating books like these into a collection shows families that we are aware and respectful, particularly if they can borrow the books to use at home with their children. Invite families to suggest additional books to use with children, and encourage their comments.

It can be interesting to all children to hear a familiar story in a language other than English.

Appropriate use of fantasy elements

As discussed in Chapter 3, folk and fairy tales must be chosen and shared with caution. Some of these stories may be frightening to toddlers who are working hard to understand the differences between reality and fantasy. Many adults remember with pleasure traditional stories like Goldilocks and the Three Bears or The Three Little Pigs. But for many toddlers these stories can be overwhelming, although they may become more enjoyable as the children grow and learn to differentiate what is real from what is imaginary. Pay close attention to children's reactions to see if the fantasy elements are appropriate, and adapt the story as necessary so that it is interesting but not scary. The language used in many fairy tales—such as "Once upon a time" or "Long, long ago"—may help to reassure older toddlers that the story is safe because it happened in the past. As children become more experienced with such stories, they will start to equate this language with fantasy.

Being cautious when selecting books does not mean that fantasy should never be used with toddlers. Indeed, some of the best books are built on gentle imaginings. Toddlers relish the adventures of likeable characters, such as those of Mr. Gumpy and his animal friends in *Mr. Gumpy's Outing*, by John Burningham. The idea of one man taking a lot of animals for a ride in a boat is pure fantasy, as is Mr. Gumpy's invitation to the animals to join him in his home for tea! Acquiring vocabulary and a basic understanding of reality versus imagination provides a background of knowledge that makes it increasingly possible for children to enjoy fantasy. For example, knowing that Mr. Gumpy really could not take all of those animals for a ride in his boat and then home to tea makes it possible for children to understand the humor in the story.

Small doses of fantasy can be absorbing and fun. But a little can go a long way. Your intimate understanding of a child is especially important in choosing the type of fantasy book that is right for him or her and determining how often that book should be shared. Depending on the child, you might even decide that fantasy should wait until the child is a little older.

Excellent artwork

Choose books with high-quality illustrations or photographs. The illustrations are often the heart of a picture book, so the more clarity they have, the more likely it is that the book will be meaningful and appealing to children and adults (Jalongo 2004). A few of the excellent illustrators of books for infants and toddler are Karen Katz (*Counting Kisses* and *Toes, Ears, & Nose!*), Eric Carle (*The Very Lonely Firefly* and others), and Laurel Molk (*Off We Go!*, written by Jane Yolen).

Concept or information books should also have high-quality and engaging pictures, whether they are photographs, artwork, or hand drawings. *What Do Wheels Do All Day?*, written by April Jones Prince with artwork by Giles Laroche, has fascinating collages of wheels, which illustrate and enhance the informative text. Any toddler who is interested in things with wheels will enjoy this book.

Although judging the quality of illustrations is a subjective process, keep in mind this characterization of high-quality illustrations, from Annis Duff's *Bequest of Wings: A Family's Pleasures with Books*:

> The striking characteristic of the pictures in the really good books . . . is that they show with intensified clarity, and with beauty, vitality, humor and charm, the things a child is likely to see in everyday experience. They invest these ordinary things with the brightness of an artist's vision. (Duff 1944, 25)

Discussion Starter

Choose a favorite picture book, either a favorite of yours or of the children in your program. Consider the following questions, from Mary Renck Jalongo's *Young Children and Picture Books*, 2d. ed. (2004) as you examine the illustrations or photographs:

1. Are the illustrations and text synchronized?
2. Does the mood expressed by the artwork (humorous or serious, rollicking or quiet) complement that of the story?
3. Are the illustrative details consistent with the text?
4. Could a child get a sense of the basic concepts or story sequence by looking just at the pictures?
5. Are the illustrations or photographs aesthetically pleasing?
6. Is the printing (clarity, form, line, color) of good quality?
7. Can children view and review the illustrations, each time getting more from them?
8. Are the illustrative style and complexity suited to the age level of the intended audience?

Based on Huck et al. (2000), in Jalongo (2004, 35)

Books in a series

Toddlers may enjoy experiencing books that are part of a series because they like meeting up with familiar characters again and again (Bardige & Segal 2005). For example, the *Hairy MacLary* series, by Lynley Dodd; the *Mr. McGee* series, by Pamela Allen; and the *Spot* books, by Eric Hill, feature characters that toddlers enjoy becoming familiar with and encountering in new situations. When adults notice that a toddler has enjoyed a book about Spot or Hairy MacLary or Mr. McGee, for example, they can share another book from the series with the child. Some children show their delight in these serial stories and characters by asking to hear them over and over.

Availability of accompanying narration

Some of the finest picture books are also available in the form of audiobooks (tape or CD) or videos (VHS or DVD) read by professional narrators and storytellers with the expression and timing to appeal to young children (and many adults!). The classic *Goodnight Moon*, by Margaret Wise Brown, for example, is available as an audiobook. Good quality readings, when used in conjunction with the actual book, give children a complete book experience. These readings are especially valuable for children with visual impairments. They offer children a new voice other than their parents or caregivers through which to hear the story or enjoy the book. (Ways to use these formats effectively are discussed in Chapter 5.)

Sturdiness and safety

Include many sturdy board books in your collection that children can use independently. Keep in mind that most of the books in your collection will need to withstand repeated use by very young children who are still learning how to handle the objects in their environment. Infants and toddlers will want to explore books by manipulating, smelling, tasting, squeezing, flapping, and carrying them in addition to turning the pages and looking at the pictures. It is inevitable that books will be damaged through children's enthusiastic use of them. However, we can prevent some degree of damage by selecting books designed for rough handling by very young children, and we can be ready to repair the damage that inevitably will occur.

Keep in mind that most of the books in your collection will need to withstand repeated use.

Aside from a few special books chosen for adults to share carefully with children, which are not available for children's independent use, be sure that the books in your collection are safe for children to use on their own. Check that the bindings are secure, that there are no small parts that could be swallowed, and that there are no sharp edges or corners. Books with metal or plastic spiral bindings are not appropriate, as young children put everything in their mouths and could hurt themselves. A chunky board book is ideal, as it would be almost impossible for such a book to become a choking hazard, unlike a paper book, from which a determined infant could bite off a wad of pages. Even fabric books designed for infants may have buttons or ribbons that could be pulled off and swallowed.

Discussion Starter

1. What is your favorite book for very young children?
2. What do you like about it?
3. How does it measure up to the criteria discussed in this chapter?

Special qualities that adults can share

Although we should take precautions regarding sturdiness and safety, it is appropriate to have some special, less sturdy books that are not accessible for children's independent use and are brought out only when an adult is available. Some hardcover books with paper pages might fall into this category, as well as some books with flaps, pop-ups, fold-out pages, or other elements that can be easily destroyed. One of the values of having these special books in a collection is that they offer a wonderful opportunity for adults to model proper care of books, treating them as something special while the child watches.

Cautions

In addition to the above criteria, consider these cautions as you build your collection of books:

1. Increasingly, books that were originally written and designed for children older than 3 years of age are being published in board book form. Often, this results in board books that are too complicated with too much text for very young children, even though the board book materials are designed just for this age group. As always, there are no hard and fast rules for deciding which books are suitable for particular children and which are not. For example, the board book *Owl Babies,* by Martin Waddell, might seem unsuitable for very young children. Yet to some caregivers, this story about three baby owls whose mother leaves and then returns to them is not only understood but about a theme welcomed by toddlers.

2. Conversely, some books with content that is appropriate and written for toddlers have been reissued by publishers as Big Books. This format is designed to be read by an adult in front of a group of children, as the large size makes it possible for a whole group of children to see the pictures. But they are not ideal for use with very young children for several reasons. If read as intended with a group of children sitting in front of the book as it is read by an adult, then they are completely inappropriate, as stories should not be shared with very young children in a large group setting. With one or two children, their size is very awkward, and children end up too close to the images. And young children cannot look at them independently without tearing them.

3. Take care when choosing books that were personal favorites from your own childhood. If you remember them well, they likely were favorites of yours when you were older than 3. Similarly, exercise caution when including books that are your current favorites. Although books such as *Love You Forever,* by Robert N. Munsch, might be particularly touching and engaging for adults, they are often less relevant—and less interesting—for young children.

Guides for selecting books

For additional guidance in choosing high-quality books, review lists of books nominated for awards and librarians' choice lists. To stay up-to-date on new resources, visit reputable book stores and ask for recommendations of new books suitable for children 3 and under. Visit book Web sites and read reviews from caregivers and parents. The more familiar you get with children's books, the easier it will be to find the very best ones for infants and toddlers. One great place to start is with the Web site of the Association for Library Service to Children, a part of the American Library Association (www.ala.org/ala/alsc). This site has helpful resources, such as "Books to Grown On," a list of books for children ages 0–3, broken down by age groups. There is also information on online children's libraries and a resource section geared toward educators.

For a list of all the children's books mentioned in this book, plus others of value, see Appendix B.

Recognizing the value of books, learning about the types available, and reviewing guidelines for building a collection are necessary first steps to maximizing story experiences for very young children. But how can we ensure that we use books, as well as other kinds of story experiences, effectively? That's the key question answered in the next chapter.

5

Using Stories Effectively
Telling, Reading, and Showing

I think you'll discover that the more stories you tell,
the more confidence you'll gain.
—Pete Seeger and Paul Dubois Jacobs, *Pete Seeger's Storytelling Book*

Let's assume that now we have a good collection of books on hand; we have a learned a repertoire of songs, language games, and oral stories; and we feel reasonably sure of our ability to share them with infants and toddlers. How can we most effectively use story experiences? As folk singer and storyteller Pete Seeger suggests, it takes practice to do it well. But with practice will come the confidence and expertise we need to ensure children get the extraordinary pleasures and benefits of language in use from our programs.

Dos and don'ts for sharing story experiences

The way we use stories is as important as the stories themselves. Infants and toddlers come to a story experience—whether told or read, original or not, musical or physical, initiated by the child or by the adult—with few if any preconceived notions about what that experience *should* be like. This gives us plenty of room to be creative and imaginative.

Within that flexibility, there are some factors to keep in mind. By accounting for what children are like and what they can do at this age (as described in Chapter 2), we make the story experiences we share with them as enjoyable and productive as possible.

Using Stories Effectively

Allow freedom and choice

Participation in story sharing should not be compulsory for very young children. Children should be invited to join in, and if they are interested in participating, they will let us know. They may also let us know which story they are interested in. Of course, an infant or toddler may show "interest" in ways very different from how an adult would, and that interest can be both brief and changeable. For example:

> In the toddler room, Lucas sets the new books for his group out on a low table and waits quietly. Two-year-old Denise wanders to the table, picks up a book, and brings it to Lucas, saying excitedly, "Book! Book!" Lucas responds by sitting on the rug and beginning to read the book to Denise. Two other toddlers run to join them and are interested and pleased by the story.

> On a walk to the park, Sandra starts singing, "There's a little white duck swimming in the water!" The toddlers listen in silence, but after they return to their room, Cheyenne grins at Sandra and says, "Sing quack quack!"

Try to share stories with children throughout the day, not only during a fixed period in the schedule. Initiate them when the situation seems right, and make time when children do the initiating. For example:

> Donny, age 22 months, approaches his caregiver with a book tucked under his arm. Squatting next to her, Donny puts the book on the floor and leafs through it until he comes to a page with a picture of a tricycle on it. He points to the picture, giving her a big grin. "I see it, Donny!" she says, "That's just like our trike!" His apparent mission accomplished—sharing with her a picture of relevance to him, and getting her to acknowledge their connection—Donny grins again and goes off, leaving the book behind on the floor.

Adjust expectations to fit children's abilities and preferences

Our understanding of child development should, in principle, inform when we share stories and which stories we select. For example, a hungry child will not usually be interested in a story, even if that story is one of her favorites. A toddler busy pushing his doll in the stroller will probably not want to stop for a story, either. And even if it seems like the optimal time for sharing a story, when distractions seem minimal, toddlers often will wander away if they are not ready for the type of story being shared or if something else captures their attention. But there are ways to integrate stories into even a busy moment:

> Anna has tried hard to interest the young toddlers in her room to sit together for a brief story before lunch, but invariably one or two get up and wander away. Anna changes the routine to singing, "This is the way we wash our hands," while the children get washed and ready for lunch. She finds that the children enjoy this and participate with delight.

Keep story groups small and intimate

Since one of the key benefits of sharing stories with infants and toddlers is fostering close relationships among the story participants, it is best to share stories with no more than three children at a time, so everyone can nestle close. Keeping groups small also allows each child to be an active participant. One or even a very few children can join in a story's refrain without being too noisy or disruptive for the other children in the room. Small groups also make it easier to maintain children's interest through eye contact and gentle touches. Larger groups are likely to require the adult to spend more time keeping order than sharing the story, which takes away from the enjoyment.

Progression of a young child's learning to use books

- Looks attentively at pictures in a book
- Recognizes a particular book
- Is able to turn the pages of a board book
- Points to pictures in a book
- Holds a book right side up
- Looks at a book from front to back, or whatever way is appropriate for the language in which the book is written and the culture from which it comes
- Recognizes a book by the cover
- Has a favorite story or book
- Makes comments about pictures in books
- "Reads" the words in a book (telling the story by looking at the pictures)
- Uses a word or phrase that clearly comes from a book or story with which the child is familiar
- Indicates that an adult reading a book has left out or added some words or skipped a page in a favorite story
- Predicts what might happen next or what the book is about from looking at the cover
- Tells a simple story
- Pretends to be "reading" to other children, or to a doll or teddy
- Takes notice of letters and words in a book by pointing to them or asking about the print

Based on Schickedanz (1999).

Show pleasure and enthusiasm

Our attitude as we share stories is critical if we want these experiences to be successful for infants and toddlers. Very young children are influenced greatly by our behavior, and they are keen observers of what we do and say. If we are enthusiastic, interested, and clearly enjoying the story, children will be more likely to feel these things, too. Pleasure is contagious—and so is boredom:

> Rhiannon, in the infant room, loves to play with and sing to the infants but believes sharing books with them is a waste of time. When asked about her avoidance of story sharing, she demonstrates to the director that when she picks up an infant to read to him, he wriggles and is "not interested in the book." The director explains that a liking for books is catching and works with Rhiannon to find some books she enjoys and can share with enthusiasm.

Be expressive

Being expressive when sharing a story helps young listeners engage with what they are hearing. Being expressive might mean using a soft voice for a gentle bedtime story such as Mem Fox's *Time for Bed*, or making your voice loud and growling like a tiger when telling a story about zoo animals. This also entails changing your tone of voice or accent for different characters. Another part of being expressive is using gestures, facial expressions, and body language in ways that support the storytelling. If young children are accustomed to hearing expressive language, they will use it themselves when they begin to tell their own stories.

Use props

Story sharing can be enriched with the careful use of props or other supplementary resources. However, props are not necessary for every story and can sometimes be distracting. For example, a teacher might introduce a large puppet to tell the story of the Little Red Hen; but if the children are more interested in the puppet than the story, then the prop might not be adding to the story experience itself. Used sensibly, props can help support very young children's participation and understanding. For example:

> Erica didn't think she needed to use her monkey finger puppet when sharing the delightful book *Monkey and Me*, by Emily Gravett, as the illustrations in the book were ideal for very young children.

However, she decided the next day to tell an adapted story of *Monkey and Me* without using the book. For this, she had the monkey puppet perform some actions to help her toddlers to follow along as she told the story.

Those caregivers who are not naturally compelling or expressive storytellers may find that using props helps maintain children's attention; in this capacity, props may help to foster more confidence in adults about their story abilities. Be creative with props—consider puppets, toys, items of clothing such as scarves and hats, natural objects such as feathers or shells, everyday items such as cups and toothbrushes, or other objects that are appropriate to the story. Sometimes we might hold the prop as we share the story; sometimes children can. For example, if a toddler is listening to a story about a teddy bear, holding that object can help the child to associate it with the words *teddy bear*. This is especially true for children who are learning English as a second language or children with visual impairments.

Follow children's *cues*

Children give many different cues or signs about how they like the stories we share with them. For the youngest children, those cues are likely to be conveyed through sounds and body language, such as gestures, wriggling, and facial expressions. As infants become toddlers, they can respond more explicitly, by saying things such as, "Again," "More story," and "No," or even by getting up and simply walking away.

> Jamal, a toddler, brings Nancy the Dr. Seuss picture book *The Cat in the Hat*. Nancy begins to talk about the pictures, but Jamal frowns, grabs the book, and shakes his head. He points to the first page and waits. "Oh," says Nancy, "You want me to read the whole story?" He nods, and Nancy reads the book word for word with great animation.

Whenever possible, repeat a story that children express interest in hearing again. Depending on the length of the story and children's interest level, some story sessions could be quite long, while others will be much shorter. The desire for repetition, which is valuable for building vocabulary and developing language skills, shows that children are engaged. Here, one child's excitement spreads to bring other children into a story experience:

> Sara, age 11 months, pays close attention as her caregiver Rosa sings "Itsy Bitsy Spider" to her. As the spider "crawls up the spout

Whenever possible, repeat a story that children express interest in hearing again.

again" for the third time, Sara wriggles in Rosa's lap and looks up expectantly. "You'd like to sing it again?" asks Rosa. Sara nods happily, but this time Rosa says, "Let's see if Li and Tony would like to share it with us—we have lots of room on either side of me." Li and Tony are added to the group, and the four of them begin the song again.

Conversely, persisting when children express a lack of interest works against what should be the ultimate goal: helping them learn to love stories.

Ideas for using told stories with infants and toddlers

As discussed in Chapter 3, told stories can extend the linguistic learning that happens through natural conversations and language play. *Told stories* can include simple made up stories, nursery rhymes, or simple poems, and we can hum, chant, or recite them throughout the day. Caregivers need to match told stories to children's age, interests, needs, and family contexts. Here are some practical ideas to consider:

Telling a nursery rhyme or poem as a story. Rhyming language is especially appealing to beginning language users because they like to play with sounds. Rhyming stories help young children to remember different sounds and how they are made.

Reflecting what children are doing back to them as a story. This helps children learn that words can describe tangible things that are happening. For example, as Eric is being dressed, his caregiver might say, "I know a little boy named Eric. Eric is putting on his pants and his shirt and his coat so he can go out to play."

Talking about the events of the day in story form. Any story, no matter how mundane, is engaging when told with enthusiasm and humor. For example, "As I was coming to the center today, what do you think I saw? Do you think I saw a cow wearing a skirt? Do you think I saw a fire engine playing a trumpet? Nooooo! I saw a mother duck and her baby ducklings walking toward the pond!"

Asking older toddlers to tell a story. Toddlers are developing their language skills and, as such, need opportunities to create their own stories. A caregiver might say, "Tell me a story about what your cat likes to do." Toddlers might respond with both factual and imagined elements in their stories. These simple stories can be written down and shared later with the child, the family, and other children.

Recognizing that story prompts exist in all parts of children's play environments. Whatever children are doing—pretending to put dolls to bed, building with blocks, painting, holding conversations—can become a story. For example, as two toddlers are digging in the sandbox, their caregiver starts singing a sandbox song, "Digging, digging with my spade." The song's story reflects what the children are doing and puts words to their actions using new vocabulary. Learning to express actions with words is a precursor skill to becoming a storyteller and eventually a story writer.

Using children's names in stories. Very young children love to hear stories that involve them. Hearing their own names in a story can help attract their attention and keep them engaged with the story.

Using familiar things or events as a starting point for sharing a story. The familiar is comforting and helps very young children to participate actively in a story because they know what the story is about. For example, a caregiver might tell a story about what happened when it rained suddenly before lunch time and the toddlers got wet. After the story, she could ask them about how they felt when it poured rain. This is an example of how a story connects feelings (e.g., scared, excited) to children's understandings about their experiences.

Telling more complex stories, such as simple versions of folk tales. These can be interesting and enjoyable for older toddlers. When they begin to join in saying the repeated phrases of folk tales, such as "You can't catch me, I'm the Gingerbread Man," this is a sign to adults that the children are more deeply engaged with stories.

Talking with toddlers about the feelings involved in a story. Toddlers will begin to understand that stories connect them to other people, and that feelings or emotions are an important part of participating in a story. Questions like "Was the baby bird happy or sad when his mother wasn't in the nest?" will help them learn this. Emotional enrichment is a key benefit of sharing stories, because it helps to connect the listener with the story.

Discussion Starter

Choose a picture from an information or concept book or a picture in a book or magazine that would interest young children. Think of what information you could share with them about the picture. Make up a simple story for a child you know, based on the picture, that will involve the child in telling a story with you. For example, with a picture of a cat, your story for 2-year-olds might start: "This is Silky the cat. Her fur is the softest thing in the world. One day she got lost. What do you think happened next?"

Talk with coworkers about how the technique of beginning a story and asking children to contribute their ideas might play out with the children in their groups. After trying this technique, report back. You can later try again using some of the different methods that other coworkers tried for this type of story sharing.

Ideas for using books with infants and toddlers

This section presents some helpful strategies for using books in effective ways. Although the information is divided roughly by age, these designations should not be viewed as prescriptive, but rather as a guide. As always, there will be children who show an interest in books that you might think would be "too old" or "too young" for them. Also, children with developmental delays and other special needs may prefer books intended for younger children. It's important to observe children's interests carefully and to follow their lead in choosing the stories they will enjoy, even when it means giving up on a plan you originally thought would be exciting or appropriate.

With infants

Pick a comfortable spot for you and an infant to share a book. Show the infant a book and invite her to look at it with you, or bring out a book in response to an earlier cue from the infant. An infant may point at or wave a book, or if she can crawl, she may even bring it to you. If she wishes to explore the book as an object—turning it over, flipping the pages, feeling its textures—show her how to do so. Be sure to use a sturdy book, such as a board book or one made out of fabric. As always, supervise carefully.

When the infant seems ready, point to the cover of the book and read the title, then wonder aloud as to what the book may be about. Turn the pages as slowly or as quickly as the infant seems to like. If you are sharing a book experience with more than one infant at a time, consider giving each child a book to explore as an object, each at his or her own pace. Continue making helpful comments to each infant, as Alice, a caregiver, does in the following example:

> Alice settles herself outside on a blanket under a shady tree with 8-month-old Sylvia, 10-month-old Samir, and 14-month-old Derek. Each infant wants to hold a book, and each has a particular style of using the book. Sylvia looks briefly at one or two pictures, then waves her book about, captivated by the way it moves. Samir leans over his book and intently studies a picture of a cat, uninterested in turning the page. Derek loves Eric Hill's *Where's Spot?*, the lift-the-flap book he is holding, and wants Alice to read it to him word for word while he hunts under the flaps for the hidden dog.
>
> While reading to Derek, Alice pauses to tell Sylvia, "Your book is moving around! Can you see the pages flap in the air?" Then she says, "Samir, that picture of a cat is very interesting, isn't it? Does it look like your cat at home?" Alice makes no effort to get the infants to all do the same thing or to explore their books in a particular way. Later, she will try to find more lift-the-flap books for Derek, a picture book about cats for Samir, and more sturdy board books for Sylvia.

If the infant is interested in viewing the book in its entirety, turn the pages, point out the pictures, and name and describe what is depicted. If possible, relate the pictures to something the infant has experienced: "That's a daddy going to work just like your daddy does," or "Mmm, those children are eating oatmeal . . . we had oatmeal for breakfast." Of course, if the text seems to interest the child, you can read it as written. But most of the time, you will be talking *about* the book and the illustrations, improvising and wondering aloud, to maintain the attention and concentration of the infant.

If an infant loses interest, which he will show by crying, moving away, or otherwise indicating that he is bored, don't insist on finishing the book. If one gentle attempt to regain his attention—by saying something like, "Let's see what's on the next page!"—does not work, then let the infant move on to something else. On the other hand, an infant may be so engaged that he wants to repeat the book experience. Take this as a compliment and indulge his wishes!

With younger toddlers

Young toddlers are usually more active participants in book sharing experiences than infants are. They may point to pictures, act out text, or repeat words we read from the book. But just as when you share books with infants, watch for cues from children about readiness for and interest in books and respond accordingly:

> At 14 months, Stella has never shown any interest in books, although she listens intently when her caregiver, Anna, sings, and she explores the toys in her environment with remarkable thoroughness. One day she toddles over to her caregiver, clasping a nursery rhyme book with both arms. Anna takes Stella on her lap and prepares to open the book, but Stella leafs through the pages and finds the picture that shows "This is the way we wash our hands," which is the song her group sings as they prepare for lunch. Anna wonders how Stella found the right page—but Stella is not saying!

Memorization of text and imitation of reading are important steps in emerging literacy.

Adults can initiate book sharing several times a day by suggesting or introducing a book, showing it to a child or two, and inviting children to look at the book together with them.

With older toddlers

Older toddlers, particularly those who have already had many pleasant experiences with books, are ready for more advanced book sharing. Generally, children in this age group will enjoy hearing stories with simple, short text, and they will quickly develop favorites, which they will want to hear over and over again. A book containing a nursery rhyme, poem, or song may particularly delight an older toddler, who may try to repeat the rhythmic words even if her spoken language is just becoming comprehensible.

We can summon children's interest in their favorite books by asking, "Can you find the book about the bear?" or, "Can you find the book with Jack and Jill in it?" Such questions will often send toddlers scurrying to get the book as quickly as they can—and they may remember more clearly where it is than we do!

Many 2- and 3-year-olds memorize their favorite books and can recite the words as the adult reads. The memorization of text and imitation of reading are important steps in emerging literacy. Some children are rigid about hearing the text in *exactly* the same way each time the book is read and object vigorously to any attempts to change or shorten what it says. We should respect these demands, as they indicate that children are beginning to understand that print and illustrations are predictable—that is, they are the same each time they are read or viewed. Research shows that from about 2 years of age, children are beginning to understand that the print on the pages of a book represents the story similar to how the pictures tell a story (Lancaster 2003; Makin 2006).

Despite individual variation, most 2- and 3-year-olds are able to talk about the feelings of the characters in a book. *Owen and Mzee: The True Story of a Remarkable Friendship*, by Isabella Hatkoff, Craig Hatkoff, and Paula Kahumbu, is a great book about an orphaned hippo who finds a surrogate mother in an ancient tortoise. Simple questions about the characters, such as "How did the baby hippo feel when he couldn't find his mother?" are appropriate for children in this age group. Without prompting, older toddlers may express their own feelings about the story: "I loved the mama tortoise with the baby hippo." It is important to acknowledge children's feelings with statements like, "Yes, I liked the mama tortoise, too. She was a very good mama for the baby hippo."

Older toddlers are happy to have books shared with them in what we might think of as more "traditional" ways; that is, the child sits on the caregiver's lap or by her side and listens to the story from beginning to the end. Of course, the school-age model for reading—an adult sitting on a low chair, facing a group of cross-legged children as she reads—is inappropriate for children under age 3. Instead, we should share books with no more than three children at a time.

A good place for books

Good infant and toddler programs are characterized not only by their excellent book collections, but also by how these books are set up and displayed. The space should be comfortable for quiet "book looking," storytelling, and book sharing. Ideally, such an area would be well-lit and away from noise and distraction, with soft pillows or a comfortable chair or couch. Books should be displayed so that children can view and access them easily. Of course, book experiences will not only occur in the designated book area (and, to be sure, they should not be confined to one space in the room), but the space should serve as a kind of informal headquarters, a place where children are confident that they can find books and adults who are eager to share stories with them.

Whenever possible, display books so that children can see their covers. Displaying books on racks with shallow shelves or grooves works well, though this method often takes up more space than many early childhood centers can spare. Some programs use containers with handles, allowing toddlers to carry—and sometimes dump—books around the room. Other programs use large containers, such as baskets or plastic tubs, which allow books to be stored in an upright position, thus encouraging children to flip through them and view the full front covers. Another good display technique is standing some books up on the floor, where they will be seen by children who are crawling and walking past the book area (Schickedanz 1999). Smaller containers of books can also be placed around the room, encouraging children to use books whenever they like. Children should know that books can be taken to other parts of the environment, sometimes simply as objects to carry or haul from one place to another and other times as resources for pictures and text to explore. Books can be taken outside, looked at in cribs or cots, read in the block or dramatic play corners, or even dramatized informally outdoors. For example:

> Several members of Marah's older toddler group enjoyed repeated readings of Maurice Sendak's *Where the Wild Things Are*. Marah took the book outside and encouraged the children to act out being the monsters in the book and making their fiercest faces while standing on the toddler climbing frames or marching around the paths.

Though books can be enjoyed in a variety of places, it is the small and comfortable book area that will provide the predictable, quiet space children need for quality book experiences, allowing them to be in close physical contact with their caregivers. Easy access and physical touch are integral components of sharing books and stories.

Challenges when using books with infants and toddlers

Though the benefits of sharing books with very young children are numerous, doing so is not without its challenges. Inexperienced caregivers likely will find this to be especially true. Some typical book-related challenges—and suggestions for how to confront them—follow:

An infant or toddler seems uninterested in the story. After a few gentle attempts to see if the child would like to look at a different page or change his position so that he can see the pictures more clearly, wrap up the story and try again at a later time, the next day, or with a different book.

A toddler seems interested for a little while, but then she gets up and walks away. Say something like, "We haven't finished the story, would you like to hear the rest?" This might encourage the child to stay and finish the book, but beyond that reminder or invitation, she should be allowed to leave.

A child has chosen a book that turns out to be too long and complicated for him. If a toddler is losing interest, try telling him the story in your own words, using the pictures as a guide, or simply talk about the pictures.

You are unable to read the book because a toddler wants to hold it and keep it in front of herself. Point to the print and say, "If you want me to read the story, I have to be able to see the words." If that doesn't work, try talking about the pictures with the child.

The child keeps interrupting with comments or questions. If you are reading to that child alone, stop to respond to the comments and answer the questions. If a couple of other children are also participating, respond briefly and say that you can talk more about the child's questions at the end of the story.

Two or three children want to sit on your lap at the same time. Allow children to take turns sitting on your lap. Then encourage the others to snuggle in on either side of you. Reading to more than three children at a time makes it impossible for all children to comfortably maintain physical contact with you.

A child wants to look at the book from back to front. Try saying something to encourage the child to look at the book in a more "traditional" way, such as, "We usually begin here," and point to the front of the book. Be flexible, though, and when possible, go with the child's preference. Another advantage of sharing books with one child at a time is that this kind of accommodation can be made. If more than one child is involved, you may have to say, "You can look at that book in your way. I am going to read this book from the front to the back." This way, all the children have a better chance of enjoying a book experience.

A child handles a book roughly. Part of our job as effective caregivers is to help very young children learn to use books and other materials properly. When a child misuses a book, say something along the lines of, "We need to be very careful with books so we can look at them many times. Let me show you how to hold it carefully and how to turn the pages so we can read the book again and again." If he persists in deliberately damaging the book, remove it and say firmly, "You are not ready to take good care of this book.

Let's put it away, and you can look at this one." Then substitute a fabric or plastic book if you think that will solve the problem. Learning to handle books appropriately is like learning to wash hands or eat independently. Mastering such physical skills takes a lot of practice and a lot of patient, encouraging help from adults before children can perform independently.

A child never initiates book experiences or seems uninterested when invited to participate. Observe the child's interests and try to find a book that reflects them. Saying, "Look! I found a picture of a fire engine just like the one you use with the blocks!" might encourage a reluctant child to share a book with you. When looking at books, encourage the child to participate by letting her turn the pages or manipulate special features, such as flaps in a lift-the-flap book (Jalongo 2004). Sharing stories with an individual child rather than with a small group is wise if the child needs particular encouragement.

Using stories: Questions from caregivers

As you think about how to use the various types of stories with infants and toddlers, you may have many questions. Often, caregivers face conflicting requests or pressure from other adults to use stories in ways that might be inappropriate. Some of these questions are featured in this section.

"How do I decide what story to tell or book to share?"

Trust your professional judgment! Your knowledge and experience guide story selection choices for particular purposes, times, and children. Your decision about what story or book to share should be based on the following:

- knowledge of the children's developmental stages, interests, strengths, needs, and family contexts;
- recognition of children's diverse ways of responding to and communicating their interest in or enjoyment of particular stories;
- knowledge of what stories are available or can be created for a particular purpose;
- understanding that while some selections might not work for unexpected or unexplainable reasons, it doesn't mean that you should stop sharing stories altogether; and
- knowledge of the books and stories the children have already enjoyed, so you can plan for what should come next.

"Should I expect toddlers to sit still when sharing a story with them?"

Some of the difficulties encountered in sharing books with toddlers come from inappropriate expectations for their behavior. Caregivers may wonder if allowing toddlers to stand up, reach for a book, interrupt, or walk away during story sharing means that children are learning patterns of behavior that will be at odds with how they will be expected to behave when they are older. But a lot of learning comes as children mature, even in a span of a few months. Right now the emphasis should be on helping children enjoy stories, rather than emphasizing what will be expected of them in the future. Because toddlers are working hard to develop their independence and are not generally interested in participating in groups, it is a good idea to allow them to express that independence instead of insisting on their full attention.

"Should I compel toddlers listen to stories or look at books?"

While sharing stories is extremely important, very young children should never be forced to listen to them. Insisting that toddlers listen to stories can work against the goal of teaching children to love books and stories. But how should you respond if, for example, a parent voices anxiety about your approach? Some parents may wonder if their children will be ready for preschool if they are not taught to sit and listen as members of a group from a young age. You can assure parents that if toddlers learn that books are sources of immense satisfaction, they will move easily into understanding that "big kids" listen to stories quietly and attentively.

"How should I use stories with children whose home language is not English?"

Children with little or no knowledge of English will generally enjoy the same stories as children who are native English speakers, provided that you are expressive and use props when you share them. Be sure to share books in the child's home language, too. Many well-known books are available in other languages or in both English and another language (see Chapter 4 for more on this subject). These can be used with all the children in the program.

"What should I do if the children want to interrupt the story?"

Young children will show their interest in something by making immediate or spontaneous connections to something they already know or have experienced. A story may trigger that kind of reaction, which means their interruptions are not always signs of a lack of attention. These interruptions may in fact signal the opposite: They are connecting with the story. Gently acknowledge their comments, and suggest that they might like to listen to what is going to happen next. Offer to talk more with them about their questions or comments after the story is finished. For example:

> Maurice is reading *Hattie and the Fox*, by Mem Fox, to three older toddlers. He shows them the first page and reads Hattie the Hen's line, "Goodness gracious me! I can see a nose in the bushes!" One of the children, Ben, exclaims, "Dat fox, fox!" Maurice smiles and replies, "Are you sure there is a fox in the bushes, Ben? Let's see if that's true, and what Hattie will do next."
>
> Ben's interruption connects to his previous experience with this story. He remembers that there is a fox in the bushes and he spontaneously expresses this knowledge. Maurice respects his knowledge and recognizes his comment but also provides a reason for Ben to keep listening.

"Can infants and toddlers be trusted with books?"

It's discouraging to hear caregivers say, "Oh, we tried giving books to our infants, but they just chewed them and tore them up. They're too young for stories." Equally discouraging is visiting a toddler room and seeing books stored where children can't reach them. We need to accept that a child will need a lot of practice and a lot of patient, encouraging help before she can master the physical skill of taking good care of books. Part of the caregiver's job is to help very young children learn to use educational materials, and books are among the most important of these. Yes, there will sometimes be damage to books, but most children will learn quickly that tearing or handling them roughly spoils them.

"What should I do if a child does not seem to like stories?"

While it's true that a few children do not seem to enjoy stories, most come to see them as sources of delight if they are offered regularly with enthusiasm and are integrated naturally into the day's experiences. You can try different types of stories to see which ones arouse a child's interest. Some children prefer concept books, others will enjoy a told story about themselves, and some enjoy poems and rhymes before they are interested in sharing more traditional stories. Try using stories which allow more interaction, such as lift-the-flaps, or let children turn the pages so they are more engaged (Jalongo 2004). Sharing stories with an individual child, rather than with a small group, is wise when a child seems uninterested in stories.

Supporting inclusion of children with special needs

All children have a right to the pleasures and benefits of stories. It is not surprising, though, that we are sometimes uncertain about how to share books and stories with young children who have special needs, as there is too little information available on doing so with children under 3 years of age (Katz & Schery 2006). Following are practical suggestions for supporting inclusion when sharing books and stories.

Children with visual impairments

Provide books, either homemade or purchased, that feature textures or smells. Give children time to explore the book through touch and smell before reading it to them. Make sure recorded stories (e.g., books, songs, poems) are readily available on CDs or tapes. Focus the child's attention on a book prior to sharing the story, and provide extra information if useful. Say, for example, "This book is about an elephant with big ears. Do you have ears? Yes, you have one ear on this side of your face and one ear on the other side," and guide the child's hands to her ears (Katz & Schery 2006; Erickson et al. 2007).

Children with hearing impairments

When sharing a story, make sure that children can focus on visual cues, such as pictures or props. Usually, your lap will be the best place for this. Use realistic pictures, photographs, or objects as visual markers for the story. Act out simple stories to reinforce their sequences and plots. The children do not need to speak dialogue or words when they act out the story and neither does the caregiver (Mitchell 2004).

Act out simple stories to reinforce their sequences and plots.

Children with attention difficulties

The strategies for sharing books and stories discussed throughout this chapter can be used with all children, including those with attention disorders. Particularly useful strategies include:

- sharing stories with no more than three children at a time;
- choosing books that concern a child's particular interests;
- being expressive, interested, and enthusiastic when sharing a story;
- sharing many types of stories to find which ones are most captivating for the child;
- having realistic expectations for what the story experience will entail and how children will react; and
- encouraging active participation (this can be verbal, such as joining in on a refrain, or physical, such as using actions or props at appropriate times).

Above all, we must be sensitive, perceptive, and flexible as we work to share the joys and benefits of books and stories with all children.

Discussion Starter

Select one of your favorite books for infants or toddlers.
1. What do you like about this book?
2. How have you used this book with infants and toddlers?
3. What different responses have children had to this book?
4. Why would you recommend this book to other caregivers?
5. After reading this chapter, would you share this book any differently than you did before? If so, how?

Every day, we make decisions about what stories to select and how they should be shared with children. These decisions depend on our knowledge of child development and of the individual children in our care, as well as on our familiarity with storytelling and children's books. But effective story experiences also require careful planning, which is addressed in the next chapter.

"Mary had a little lamb, its fleece was white as snow, and everywhere th

6

Planning Story Experiences to Benefit Every Child

Preparation, Observation, and Evaluation

Stories can illustrate and illuminate, cause us to wonder and confirm what we already know.
—Margie Carter, *Exchange Every Day*

For every child in our care to get the most out of the story experiences we provide takes planning—to ensure that those experiences are enjoyable, interesting, and appropriate given each child's interests, strengths, challenges, and family background. Chapter 2 provided a good summary of what very young children typically know and can do at various ages and stages in their development and learning. That gives us a starting point for planning story experiences. But to meet every child's individual needs means we must add to that general knowledge a caregiver's intimate understanding of the particular children in the program, and use that understanding in an intentional way.

Planning consists of three interwoven processes, each informing the others, all ongoing and continuous. To plan effectively, we must *prepare* by gathering materials, setting up the environment, practicing our story skills, and building a ready repertoire of story experiences to draw on. We must *observe* how each child participates in and responds to a story. And we must *evaluate* how the story experience went, as the basis for revising our plan and making new ones for next time.

Planning requires us to think ahead; some story experiences will be more planned than others, but that does not mean that sharing stories with

Noticing very young children

We learn about children by carefully watching them, listening to them, and studying their work. Watching and listening to them helps us understand what they are feeling, learning, and thinking. Here are four guidelines to help you be an effective observer:

Observe over time. Observing the same child over time enables you to see that child change and grow.

Watch children in varied situations. Like you, children may act differently according to the situation. Such factors as the social setting, time of day, individual preferences, degree of choice, and level of competence may influence a child's behavior.

Keep track of what you see. This will help you become a more intentional observer, notice patterns, and obtain a more complete picture of the child.

Observe in and out of the action. Don't limit yourself by thinking that you can only observe when you step out of the action. Observe while participating in the action, reflect on the action after the fact, and/or make some notes.

Reprinted, with permission, from Jablon, Dombro, & Dichtelmiller (2007).

infants and toddlers is always best as a structured, scheduled activity. It is fine to set aside specific times to share stories in specific ways—to sing quiet lullabies at naptimes, for example. But story sharing with very young children should not be limited only to those times and those ways. A very young child's natural unpredictability also makes it developmentally inappropriate to insist or even expect that a story experience occur at a certain time or in a certain format.

However, we can't count on appropriate and pleasurable story experiences to just happen. Story opportunities often arise spontaneously. But our job is to arrange the environment and the circumstances to make such opportunities more likely. Also, we must be able to recognize when an opportunity does present itself, and then have the skills and resources to make the most of it.

To see what good planning looks like in practice, let's make an imaginary visit to the family child care home of Steve and Ayesha:

> Steve, Ayesha, and the four children in their care take a walk every morning. Today they visit the nearby lake. To the children's delight, they see a mother duck with a line of ducklings swimming behind her! Steve carries a small digital camera on all their group excur-

sions, and he snaps a few photos. The children are full of comments, questions, and observations, which the adults closely attend to. Micah, age 2, quacks loudly, eliciting chuckles and waves from 14-month-old Julie in the stroller. After several minutes, the ducks swim out of sight. Jeremy and Lulu, both 3, want to come back later with food for the ducks. Ayesha suggests, "How about we try to return tomorrow with some bread?"

Already Steve and Ayesha have demonstrated several principles of effective story planning. They have arranged a setting (the daily walk) in which the children are likely to encounter interesting events and objects worthy of comment and conversation. Although the arrival of the duck family is unanticipated, Steve has come prepared with his camera and so is able to document the event.

Most important, the adults recognize a great opportunity for story experiences:

Back at the house, Steve helps the children wash up for snack while Ayesha rummages quickly through the bookshelves and the equipment closet, pulling out a wordless picture book with ducks on one page and a copy of the classic *Make Way for Ducklings,* by Robert McCloskey. She also finds a yellow rubber duck fresh from the dishwasher.

Steve sits down on the floor with the toddlers to look at the wordless book, while Ayesha takes Julie for a diaper change. As she changes Julie, she sings, "There's a little white duck sitting in the water . . . " while Julie chews on the duck toy. Steve talks about the pictures in *Make Way for Ducklings* with the three toddlers and discusses with them how "their" ducks are similar to or different from the ducks in the story.

At the lake, Steve and Ayesha note the children's interest and delight in the ducks, and once back home they extend and enrich the encounter with duck-related picture books, a song, and more conversation.

In the afternoon, Steve suggests the children write a story about their morning adventure. Jeremy and Lulu dictate, "We saw a mommy duck and her babies. They were swimming. We are going to see them again tomorrow." Micah quacks loudly, and Steve adds to the story, "The mommy duck said, 'Quack, quack!'"

Steve puts out the paper and fingerpaints and suggests the children make pictures about the water in the pond and the ducks, which they do with enthusiasm and much discussion. While the children nap, he prints out the photos he took at the lake, and Ayesha posts the children's dictated story and the photos for their families to see. At the end of the day she also hands each child his or her painting, suggesting that on the way home the family member ask, "Tell me a story about your painting."

Though the adventure the children have on their walk is spontaneous, Steve and Ayesha are prepared to work the event into a story experience that will continue to foster the children's interest. They document the duck encounter by taking photos and help the children to be authors of their own duck story. Steve carefully captures all their ideas, including Micah's "quacks." Steve and Ayesha make sure to share the story and photos, understanding that sharing children's experiences with families not only strengthens the bonds between child and parent, but also develops trust and encourages communication between caregivers and families.

That evening, Ayesha and Steve look for more books with ducks in them. They also investigate some other topics that each specific child seemed interested in, such as floating. They remind each other about a couple of poems and songs that mention ducks or could be modified to do so. Ayesha finds a field guide to birds so they can identify the mother duck if she is visible when the children next visit the lake. Steve adds the photos of the children watching the ducks to their written story. He glues the pages together into a book, complete with a cover that says "Our Duck Story, by Jeremy, Julie, Lulu, and Micah," which the children will be able to revisit tomorrow and add to over time.

Finally, Ayesha and Steve base their plans for the following day on the duck experience and the children's reactions to it. They look for additional resources; and because they have observed the children carefully, they are able to select follow-up stories to suit each individual's interests, ones that will both satisfy and extend the children's curiosity.

Although not every day contains the opportunity for such rich story experiences, it is a rare day in an early childhood program when children do *not* make discoveries that reveal their interests and suggest their competencies. In this chapter, we examine the different aspects of planning and its relation to meeting every young child's individual needs and interests.

Imagine that you are a caregiver for a group of 2-year-olds. Several of the children have become interested in taking off and trying to put on their shoes, which they do several times each day for several days. Think about the steps that Ayesha and Steve took in the vignette as you discuss the following questions:

1. How will you share stories related to this new interest? What other experiences will you plan to provide?

2. What printed resources will you share with the children to enrich their understanding of shoes and other types of footwear? If you are not familiar with books related to this interest, where will you turn for suggestions?

3. What poems and songs related to shoes and getting dressed will you share with the toddlers? Can you alter the words of a well-known rhyme or song so that it fits with the children's interest in shoes?

4. How might you capture the children's play, talk, and stories about shoes for your own planning purposes? To share with families?

Balancing considerations in story planning

As discussed in the preceding chapters, planning needs to support young children's participation in and love for stories through developmentally appropriate and culturally sensitive practices, carefully prepared environments, and a variety of well-chosen resources. That means finding just the right combination of elements. Following are some examples of this complex balancing act.

The familiar and the new

Very young children can feel overwhelmed emotionally and mentally if there is too much novelty, but they will be bored if nothing ever changes. They are likely to feel more secure when familiar experiences are presented as the base upon which new and unfamiliar experiences are built. Starting with the familiar and stepping toward new experiences broadens children's horizons while reinforcing and extending existing knowledge.

Knowing this, we should plan to keep some favorite books on the shelves and add new ones from time to time. Familiar nursery rhymes, poems, or other told stories that the children have enjoyed should also be offered again and again, along with new told stories. This type of balanced planning means that stories will both meet very young children's need for familiarity and provide the opportunity for them to discover and be stimulated by new things.

Thoughtful decisions about which books to remove from the shelves and which new ones to make available, or which told stories to repeat and which to add to the repertoire, are based on observations of the children's current interests as well as the particulars of the child care program. The following vignette shows how one caregiver makes a thoughtful planning decision about the books to make available to the infants in her program:

> Sue works in the infant room in a child care center. In this room, there is a small cozy space where sturdy books and other printed materials are available for the infants to explore. Every two weeks she reviews the books that are available in this space and checks them against her notes about the infants' current interests, skills, needs, and history of participation in the stories that their caregivers have shared with them.
>
> During one of her planning sessions, Sue realizes that during the next two weeks, the infants will face a difficult time because two of their regular caregivers will be away. She had intended to remove most of the familiar books and introduce new ones. However, because Sue knows that the absence of familiar caregivers may be unsettling for the children, she decides to remove only one or two of the books. Also, she leaves lots of the familiar and favorite books on display, which she hopes the children will find reassuring.

Good planning involves providing a variety of interesting and enjoyable story experiences in a manageable way.

Order and variety

Variety is essential for meeting the diversity of children's interests, strengths, and needs as story participants and later as storytellers. Chapters 3 and 4 described the many, many different kinds of story experiences and materials we can use with infants and toddlers. The multitude of choices can be almost overwhelming. Good planning involves providing a variety of interesting and enjoyable story experiences in a manageable way.

For example, it is important to balance children's need for independence and freedom with the need for order, so that books can be found, shared, and cared for appropriately. One way to do this is to carefully plan the layout of the storytelling area. Chapter 5 discussed how to set up this kind of space for infants and toddlers.

It is best to be very familiar with all the story resources available—to read all the books, know where the props are kept, and learn the new rhymes and finger games. Knowing what resources you have and where they are makes it easy to respond quickly and appropriately when a story opportunity arises.

Predictability and flexibility

Because very young children thrive on predictability, it may be a good idea to have at least one time period each day that infants and toddlers can count on for story sharing. But children in a program with too strong a focus on scheduling or programming in a story experience at a specific time each day are missing out on a lot. One regularly scheduled story sharing event cannot compete in richness and delight for the children with a program infused with singing, reading, reciting rhymes or chants, telling stories, and sharing books throughout the day.

Adults who work well with infants and toddlers are always thinking about how to introduce, enrich, and extend story and other language experiences, always using them in natural ways that encourage children to see them as vital parts of everyday life. The needs and interests of the children, the weather, the mood of the group, any unexpected and sometimes delightful event can suggest a story, poem, or song.

Maintaining this kind of flexibility does not mean there is no order or consistency to the routines of the day; young children feel safest when they know what comes next. But if there is an exciting event—say an unexpected snow flurry in the middle of the morning—caregivers should be able to respond to children's interest and delight. Instead of introducing a new concept book as originally planned, we might pull out the classic picture book *The Snowy Day*, by Ezra Jack Keats. Similarly, if a group of infants sees a large dog in the park when they take a morning walk, we could sing "BINGO" and tell a story about our own dog.

Stories can be linked to children's experiences—the way Steve and Ayesha linked *Make Way for Ducklings* to the ducks they and the children saw at the lake. And the reverse is true, too. In other words, sometimes children's interest in a story will lead us to think of other kinds of experiences we can link to, helping children see connections between their own experiences and the experiences described in a story. For example, after sharing the humorous and beautifully illustrated book *Flower Garden*, by Eve Bunting, a caregiver might help toddlers make connections with their own gardens at home or at the center. Questions such as "Where do you have a garden at home, Mai?" or "What did we do in our garden yesterday, Ben?" can help the children connect the imaginary garden story with their own lives.

For a purpose and just because

Making these connections—if done creatively and thoughtfully—can make an integrated learning opportunity out of almost any situation. But not every experience the child has must be expanded into a lesson. Sometimes it is enough just to experience what is happening in the shared story. It isn't necessary to ask the children questions at the end of every story experience. Sometimes children will need time to think about the shared story or to look at the pictures without the interruption of questions by adults (Jalongo 2004).

Sometimes we choose a story experience simply because it will be interesting and enjoyable. For example, there are beautiful picture books with interesting content and compelling characters that should be shared with children even if the books cannot explicitly be connected to a current interest or event. You will get to know these not-to-be-missed books through sharing hundreds of stories and noting which ones generate the most enthusiastic responses from infants and toddlers. This list of books will always be growing, as excellent new books are continuously published or you hear of overlooked gems through word of mouth.

Discussion Starter

Planning for story experiences throughout the day is, in fact, a skill. If you were helping to select a new caregiver for your program, one who would value very young children's engagement with and enjoyment of stories, what answers would you want to hear to the following questions?

1. How would you foster a love for stories in the children?
2. What kinds of resources are appropriate when planning to share stories?
3. How can sharing stories help you build relationships with children?
4. How can sharing stories help support children's emerging literacy skills and understanding of language?

Planning stories as comfort and support

The physical and emotional closeness that comes from sharing a story together can give very young children a special sense of security. This makes stories valuable and useful tools for comforting and supporting children during difficult times:

- A toddler who is finding it hard to separate from his mother in the morning might be comforted by having his favorite book read to him. The book could be brought in from home (as a transition item), or it could be a favorite from the program's collection. A book on the theme of separation also could help; for example, the pictures from Audrey Penn's book for older children, *The Kissing Hand*, could be used to tell the toddler a reassuring story.

- A personal book made for a child who will be away from the program for an extended time (e.g., for a medical reason) is a good way to help her still feel connected. For example, the book might have captioned photos of familiar objects in the classroom or family care home, or labeled photos of the other children and the staff.

- Told stories can ease toddlers from one routine to another, such as coming to the rug or gathering for snack. Sharing a story at such times can help them understand that they are in transition from one experience to another, as in this example:

  > Corinne always tells this simple story when her group is readying to go outside: "All the children in Red Room have put on their coats, hats, and mittens, and now they are ready to go outside and have fun and play with each other!" The story signals the coming change from "inside" to "outside."

Stories like this one, about an upcoming event or routine, prepare children for what's going to happen next.

- Stories can help children settle into nap or rest time. Toddlers are busy, active players, and they need adult support to learn how to slow down and "switch off" so that they can rest or sleep.

- Similarly, stories with a rhyming structure or even cadence can help infants and young toddlers to ease into a calmer state, either before nap time or when they have become upset. Singing a lullaby to infants can also help them settle down for their nap time.

Reading and providing books before rest or nap time can help establish lifelong habits of reading before going to sleep. For older children, literacy experts recommend bedtime story reading, either with an adult or independently, to support literacy learning (Burns, Griffin, & Snow 1999). Though young children cannot yet do it themselves, reading before sleep is a good habit to establish early.

Developing your story planning skills

Good planning starts with being prepared. We need to be able to recognize a story sharing opportunity and be ready to seize the moment when we see one. This takes knowledge, skill, and sensitivity. Part of being prepared includes improving and extending our skills as storytellers and story participants. To develop your skills, among other things, you can:

- Regularly use professional development books such as this one to continuously build on your knowledge.
- Practice telling and reading stories with expression, especially if you are new to story sharing or not confident in your abilities.
- Take time to listen and watch children as they explore books or participate in story experiences, to learn about their interests.
- Make sure all the resources you need are at hand, enabling flexibility with story sharing.
- Demonstrate surprise, wonder, excitement, pleasure, amusement, interest, and enjoyment so that children learn what happens when you share stories with others (Zeece 2003).
- Compile planning notebooks or folders, in which your observations of story experiences with the children are recorded, along with photographs, if appropriate. You can revisit these notebooks to gain understanding: Why were the story experiences important to the children, how might they be extended, and why might they need to be repeated?

As we plan and share, we need to evaluate children's responses to the experiences we offer, and we need to think about our own sharing skills. Reflecting on what went well and what did not will help us as we continuously plan and prepare for new story sharing opportunities.

Planning story experiences for infants and toddlers allows us to build on their emerging interest in stories, enrich their learning, and aid in their development as story participants and storytellers. The greater our skill in planning, the better the experiences will be for children. But in order to offer the best story experiences, we also need to partner with children's families, which is the subject of the next chapter.

Daddy, car. . . . You're pointing at the car, Marica. Did you and your daddy ride

r? . . . Big! . . . **Yes, Marica, that building is big.**

Partnering with Families

Enriching Story Experiences Through Communication

Every family has stories and storytellers. . . . These stories help children know
who they are and where they come from.
—Betty S. Bardige and Marilyn M. Segal, *Building Literacy with Love*

Families play an important role as children learn to love stories and develop their confidence as communicators and learners. We can help families recognize opportunities for nurturing a love of stories. Some families will have stories to share that have been handed down across generations or that are an important part of their family culture, such as folk tales.

All families have their own experiences that provide excellent starting points for stories. These include both major events (moving into a new house, getting a pet, the arrival of a new baby) and everyday events (buying a new refrigerator, Dad losing his keys, visiting Grandma, celebrating holidays, going to the zoo). These family memories of shared experiences are important and, if told, will become treasured stories, contributing to a child's sense of self and strengthening his connection with his family, culture, and community.

One of the main benefits of using stories with children is that doing so strengthens relationships. When families and caregivers share stories about the child and about the family's experiences, cultural traditions, and community life, as well as the child's experiences in the program, everyone—children, families, caregivers, and the program as a whole—benefits. Relationships grow and caregivers and families learn from each other. When we communicate with families, we can and should stress the importance of stories in children's lives, and we must affirm and support families' enthusiasm and commitment to sharing them. This chapter provides tips and guidelines for partnering effectively with families.

Inclusive perspectives on families

Sharing stories and building relationships with families requires us to be aware of the beliefs and values we bring into our relationships with families. Implicit beliefs come from upbringing, experience, and training, and caregivers must sometimes work hard to recognize the ways in which their beliefs influence interactions with families.

Tolerance for and honest communication about how the caregivers' and the family's belief systems might differ are important for fostering respectful relationships with each other. We must acknowledge our own beliefs and values in order to see the different ideas that families in the program have about child care. Then we can begin to work with families to act on what they find important, finding some common ground along the way that will help everyone feel comfortable about the welfare of the children.

Families have high standards and ideals about their own children, and caregivers have a role both in affirming attitudes and beliefs already held and in helping to shape new ones. Where storytelling is concerned, for example, telling a father how much his 2-year-old son loves to listen to stories may encourage the father to begin sharing stories at home, or it may reinforce the father's standing belief that sharing stories is a worthwhile experience.

Sometimes, when values conflict, families might feel that a program fails to respect their beliefs, experiences, and knowledge (or vice versa). This can be particularly difficult if the values of other families seem to match those of the caregiver (McNaughton 2007). The challenge for us is to look beyond what is familiar and find ways to embrace the different perspectives families bring to the program. Families share language, stories, and books with their children in a variety of ways according to their cultural or community traditions (Curenton 2006). We should strive to respect and learn from these differences: Families and caregivers need to work together in partnership, for such a relationship is in the best interests of children.

The following vignette illustrates the impact of family experiences on children's understanding. It also demonstrates that caregivers can shape

Families have high standards and ideals about their own children.

From Lullabies to Literature

stories to address children's similarities and differences both sensitively and creatively:

> While using playdough one morning, 2-year-old Sean sticks a plastic straw into a lump of dough he has formed. He surveys it thoughtfully for a moment, then leans forward, blows on the straw, and sings "Happy Birthday," imitating a tradition he has participated in with his family. Intrigued, two other toddlers at the table clamor for straws and imitate Sean's actions. Eliza, their caregiver, sings with them and takes a picture of the three children with their "cakes."
>
> When the children have all gone home for the evening, Eliza glues the picture to a piece of cardboard. The next day she shows the children the picture and tells a story: "One day, Sean used dough to make a birthday cake. Dionne and Lee made cakes, too! They all blew out the candles on their cakes and sang the Happy Birthday song."
>
> Eliza then wonders whether the rest of the toddlers in her group celebrate birthdays, name days, or other special occasions. After checking with families to make sure that every child has at least one celebratory day, she posts a piece of paper by the door and asks families to briefly describe their special celebrations. Eliza turns this information into a story called "How We Celebrate Our Special Days." She uses the same formula for each child: "When [name of child] celebrates [his/her] special day, [he/she] _____!" She fills in the blanks with information the families have provided.
>
> The toddlers love this story format and ask to hear their stories often. They soon chime in with Eliza as she talks about each child. Eliza uses the center's camera to take a picture of each child listening to her describe his or her celebration. She assembles the pictures and descriptions in a photo album, which becomes one of the most popular books in the story corner of the room.

Before starting on this project, Eliza establishes that each family acknowledges celebrations, so as not to make any child feel left out or any family feel uncomfortable. Had there been a family in the group that did not endorse special occasions, Eliza would not have pursued this story activity. But by considering the different customs of the families in her program and engaging in this interactive approach to storytelling, Eliza encourages the children to value the experiences—and the stories—of others.

Two-way communication

The stories children hear and tell become more meaningful when families and caregivers communicate with each other clearly and often. As families learn more about what happens in the program, they can talk about it and encourage older, verbal children to tell stories about their time there, and as caregivers learn more about the families, they gain insight into children's interests and their lives outside the program.

When we incorporate experiences children have at home into the stories we tell in the program, we show respect for families and make stories more relevant, and thus more interesting, for very young children. We can also ask families to share their children's favorite songs, books, poems, and other stories with us. Incorporating familiar story experiences from home into the child care program can add to children's feeling of security and strengthen the bridge between home and the program.

New information about the child emerges continually as caregivers and families share their knowledge (Rinaldi 2006). For example:

> Eighteen-month-old Amy recently began attending Carla's family child care program. Though Carla met and spoke with Amy's

---

Discussion Starter

To reinforce how important a child's connection to family is, consider the following questions.

1. Tell one of your favorite stories about your own family to a friend or co-worker. How did telling the story make you feel about your own family? If your story evoked strong memories or feelings for you, maybe of pride, shame, joy, anger, or nostalgia, how did the listener help you accept and cope with your feelings—perhaps by validating your anger or augmenting your pride?

2. When you listen to children's stories about their families, how can you help them tell those stories? Remember that when very young children tell stories, they may use very few words and rely on you to fill in many of the gaps! For example, a toddler who says to you, "Mommy ouch," will need encouragement and help from you if you are to hear the whole story about how Mommy got her thumb caught in the car door. When you work with children to understand their stories about their families, you strengthen your connection with and interest in children's home lives: their family members, their activities, and their interactions.

---

mother when Amy was enrolled, Carla discovers new and useful information about Amy each time the two women talk. She finds out that Amy was cared for previously by her maternal grandmother, who lives on a farm. Carla understands more about Amy after learning this bit of information, particularly in relation to stories: Amy loves stories that have farm animals in them, especially when the storyteller incorporates animal noises.

When we work with families to support a child's development and learning, everyone finds out more about the child. Together we share perspectives and information, and as a result we can all operate with a more complete picture of the child. For example, one mother was delighted to hear from the caregiver about her toddler's intense interest in rhyming words. The mother began to play word games with him at home. She later told the caregiver, "Suddenly, it was as if we had some special brand of fun we had discovered and could enjoy together."

In summary, effective communication between caregivers and families helps all of us to:

Interpret children's behavior. For example, a caregiver will be able to understand and respond appropriately to a toddler's distress at hearing a story about a lost dog if the caregiver knows that the family dog has recently died.

Notice what we might not see otherwise. For example, a child starting to use his fingers to turn the pages of a board book rather than grabbing them with his whole hand is an exciting milestone worth sharing. If we relay this development to a family—or if a family tells us about such an event—we are all encouraged to observe children more closely and notice other fascinating behaviors that illustrate children's amazing ability to learn.

Build on children's interests. For example, if a mother tells the caregiver that her child is fascinated by water, the caregiver can know to talk with the child about his past experiences with water (e.g., when he went swimming) and can tell stories related to water (e.g., ducks splashing in the rain).

Just as we individualize our interactions with each child, so too should we individualize our communication with each family. Some families are confident about the decisions they make regarding their children, and others are not; some families are eager to receive suggestions from caregivers, while some invariably construe such comments as criticism. We should aim to nurture families' confidence and the pleasure they get in interacting with their children, through stories and other activities.

Documentation and very young children

Documenting infants' and toddlers' experiences with stories helps to make their learning visible to others (Rinaldi 2004). This is particularly important for the families of these young children, as many children in these age groups cannot yet fully relate the day's events, and there are not likely to be many physical products of their work (such as drawings or writing samples).

Documentation "invites the parents to feel close to their children's experience away from home" (Gandini & Goldhaber 2001, 132). When documentation is thought of as a way to connect families to their children's lives in child care, it becomes an act of love and caring.

Documentation of children as they enjoy and share stories and use language can be done through notes, diaries, audio tapes, photos, and videos. Documenting through photographs is an excellent way to share children's experiences with families, though the costs associated with digital cameras, scanners, and printers may be prohibitive. Borrowing some of these resources from a local library or from families may be possible.

With very young children who cannot yet talk about their learning, documentation may involve our written observations of the child's communication through body language, gestures, and behavior. For example, a panel or poster with photos of a 14-month-old engaging with a picture book might also include notes about how the child is pointing at an object on a page and making an effort to repeat sounds heard when an adult shared the book with him.

Sharing this information with families and incorporating their feedback into new plans is an ongoing process. We can collect information that families tell us about stories their children are enjoying at home and the different ways families share stories. Some families will describe how they use oral storytelling with their children, while other families might share their infants' or

Encouraging families to tell stories and share books

Some practical suggestions follow for supporting families in using stories and books with their children. These suggestions should be adapted to fit the families in your program; what is most important is to ask families what *they* would find helpful as they set out to nurture a love of stories in their children. Be prepared to act on what they say.

toddlers' favorite picture books. This information can be used when planning for story experiences in the center or family child care program (Curenton 2006).

Documentation can also be used to create new stories to share. We can, for example, take photographs of the toddler group's walk to the park. Later, we can place the photos in a sturdy blank book or on a low wall and write down the children's own words about the experience under the photographs. Ask families who speak a language besides or in addition to English to write captions for photographs or other documentation in their own language; this can be added to our comments in English.

Documenting in this way creates and preserves a story for children about their own experiences. It allows them to share, revisit, and continue learning from the event. Children may be excited to share these stories with their families, too. These shared group stories enrich the children's lives, for they help to support a sense of belonging through a shared history with the group.

Discussion Starter

1. How do you currently communicate with families about their child's interest in stories and in language in general?

2. Do families receive as much "good news" as "bad news" from you about their child's learning, development, and behavior?

3. What are three ways in which you could improve communication with families about their child's engagement with stories and their language learning?

4. How will you involve families in determining the ways in which they like to receive information about their child?

Let families know about all the ways they can use stories with very young children. Help them to value the variety of story experiences: told stories, language games, poems, songs, stories found in books, stories that are a part of the family's culture or community, and stories that are about the family specifically.

Include information about stories in your newsletter. One recurring feature of the newsletter can be an annotated list of recommended books for different age groups and interests, or a section on creative story sharing ideas to try out at home.

Let families know about the books, poetry, music, and told stories that are current favorites with children. Consider having a told story, rhyme, book, or song of the week. Just as bookstores have staff members write reviews of books, write a review of the story of the week and emphasize why it's a favorite; that is, what characteristics make it particularly attractive to the children in the group. Provide some of the children's responses to the story as well. These reviews could appear in the family newsletter, next to the list of recommended books, or on a notice board.

Organize a family night with a skilled storyteller, preferably from among the children's families. In many families, older members, such as grandparents, are excellent storytellers with wonderful stories to share. Children love hearing stories from and about their loved ones. Being able to share these stories with a group of peers will foster pride and enjoyment.

Ask families to contribute stories from their own childhoods, cultural backgrounds, or home languages to use in the program. In one center, a group of mothers from different African countries recorded traditional songs in their native languages on the center's tape recorder. These songs not only interested all the children, but the familiarity of the languages was very soothing and comforting to the children whose families spoke them at home. Incorporating greetings, songs, books, and told stories in languages other than English, as well as pictures from a variety of cultures, will benefit and delight all children.

Value each family's ability to contribute to the program. Consider how the family in the example below supports the use of stories in the child's program by drawing upon their particular talents and interests:

> Todd's parents are teenagers who are talented musicians; one plays the guitar and the other sings. They agree to share their talents with the children at the center once a week. The children are delighted to hear them sing familiar nursery rhymes and are enthusiastic about learning the new songs they introduce.

Discussion Starter

1. Have you had occasions when you had to decide between appropriateness and the value of using a story, song, or book contributed by a family member of a child in your program?
2. If so, what were the issues you considered?
3. How did you resolve the issue, and how did you feel about your decision?

Encourage families to use the public library. Ask the librarians to suggest books in their collection that are appropriate for very young children. Post an announcement for families, highlighting what is available at the library. Organize a group visit to the local library. Include information on obtaining a library card in a family newsletter. Invite a children's librarian to the program to speak to families about resources and special events.

Set up a lending library. Ensure that you offer books in the first languages of all the families in your program. A parent or grandparent may be eager to help organize a lending library. This is a great way for families to get involved.

Make up a collection of story bags. Story bags can contain an age-appropriate book or a set of nursery rhyme cards, props such as finger puppets or felt figures that can accompany the story, and suggestions for activities related to the book. Also include a sheet with general tips for sharing stories. Be available to show families how to use the story bags in case they are unsure of what to do (Anning & Edwards 2006). If possible, story bags should be available in all of the languages represented in the program. In one community, a local ethnic association agreed to fund the translation of the story bag resources. If resources are scarce, a local service club may want to sponsor these story bags. Books can also be purchased inexpensively at used bookstores.

Hold a family book sale or trade fair. This enables families to sell or trade books their own children have outgrown and add books to their collections. This inexpensive way of broadening a home library also helps bring the child care community—including families, children, and caregivers—together.

Organize a book-making workshop for families. There are few more effective strategies for sensitizing adults to the intricacies of attractive books for infants and toddlers than encouraging them to make books themselves. Such a workshop can be a valuable learning experience as well as an opportunity to build cooperation and community among participants.

Above all, talk with families about their children. Emphasize children's amazing learning capabilities and the everyday, ordinary ways that families can promote a love of stories. The chats at the beginning and end of each day are what build the relationships between families and caregivers.

General guidelines

As you work to promote families' effective use of stories, keep the following in mind:

• Start with strengths and competencies. All children, parents, families, and caregivers have them.

- Avoid burdening families with additional responsibilities. Instead, help them to take advantage of everyday opportunities for incorporating stories into children's lives. Help them to recognize the informal story sharing that they may already be doing.
- Help families to tune into and build on their children's interests. Be sure to follow up on how these interests are experienced at home.
- Reinforce that sharing stories should be fun. Encourage families to laugh together and enjoy stories together. It is easy to forget that sharing and learning with children can and should be fun.

We must help the family see not only that they *can* do a very good job, but that they probably already are. Families may be surprised and pleased to learn that their infants and toddlers love stories, and we may be equally surprised and pleased to discover the rich story experiences that very young children have at home. Encourage families to share their stories with their children, whatever those stories may be and however they may go about doing it. One of the best gifts caregivers can give to a child is supporting the child's relationship with his or her family.

All of the information about stories in this book can be shared in some way with families, and all of the experiences we offer to children are enhanced when families and caregivers are in partnership. But welcoming families and working in partnership with them does not just happen automatically; it needs to be planned, with deliberate steps taken to make partnership a reality. Only then can very young children have the best chance of experiencing and enjoying stories.

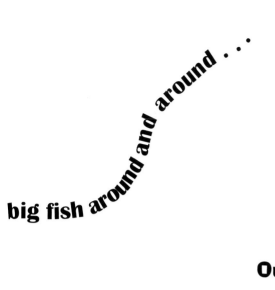

The Gift of Stories

Ours to Give to Very Young Children

Stories are how we transmit our truth, our insight, and our commitment.

—Jim Greenman, *Exchange Every Day*

Some children are fortunate to be cared for in programs where conversations, language play, and stories are a natural part of everyday experiences. These programs have caregivers who cannot imagine caring for infants and toddlers without talking to them, singing to them, telling and listening to their stories, and sharing books together. They take to heart what Betty Bardige and Marilyn Segal assert: "The stories we give to children when they are young can be lasting gifts" (2005). Such adults are skilled and passionate story participants themselves, and they share their passion with families, working in partnership with them to help every child in their care benefit from the experiences. . . . But not all children are so lucky.

This book has attempted to reach caregivers of both types—those who share stories and those who do not. If you are already immersing very young children in a steady and delightful stream of story experiences, we hope we have reinforced and encouraged your efforts. But if you counted yourself among the second type of caregiver, we hope we have succeeded in convincing you that the gift of stories can greatly improve any early childhood program.

Children's joy and interest in stories is very powerful. The tentative coo of a very young infant, made in response to a caregiver's words, can influence that adult to say more to the child, and an almost magical interaction may begin, with adult and child engaging in reciprocal vocalizations. This may prompt the caregiver to take the infant in her arms, prolonging and reinforcing their emotional connection. In the same way, the grin on a toddler's face when his caregiver plays a lap game or reads him his favorite story can have a powerful, positive influence on both adult and child. We promise the admiring, interested, and engaged responses that sharing story experiences with infants and toddlers elicits will leave you eager to share more with them. The more you share, the more you will recognize that when young children express their enthusiasm, they are giving you clues about what they want and need from you.

Questions to think about as you share stories

To determine the suitability of a story experience you are thinking of sharing with very young children, make sure you can answer yes to these questions:

1. Is it appropriate for the ages and interests of the children?
2. Does it support the attitudes and values of the program?
3. Is it culturally appropriate?
4. Is it free from stereotypes?
5. Have you familiarized yourself with the story?
6. Have you thought about how you will introduce it to the children?
7. Do you have ample time for children to ask questions and indulge their curiosities?
8. Does this fit with your program's balance of oral storytelling, language play, and books?
9. Will this experience work well for all children in your care, including those with special needs such as a vision or hearing impairment?

The three benefits of stories revisited

As we promised in our first chapter, this book about the joys and benefits of sharing stories with infants and toddlers has used the term *story* very deliberately, stretching it to cover many different kinds of verbal communications that take place between adults and children in the first three years of life. Verbal accounts of a child's daily experiences are stories, as are many nursery rhymes, folk songs, and poems. Certainly many books contain stories, and many more can be prompts for storytelling. With the term *story experience,* we sought to also capture the early language experiences that prepare the way for more conventional story participation, such as making, listening to, and reacting to sounds, songs, spoken language experiences such as rhyming and repetition, and face, lap, and knee games.

All these story experiences are most satisfying and most beneficial when they occur in a steady but ever deepening stream, beginning at birth and extending throughout life. Although the benefits of sharing stories with very young children are countless, three in particular have guided the discussion throughout this book. As this last chapter revisits those benefits, we invite you to think over what you have learned about sharing stories and how that might relate to your own program and the children with whom you work.

Stories enrich and expand children's lives

Story experiences can expand children's knowledge of the world in which they live while affirming the everyday experiences they have at home and in the early childhood program. They introduce children to the structure, rhythms, rhymes, and beauty of language. They can encourage children to use their imaginations, to giggle and laugh, and to ask questions. Stories can help them see that they are part of a world in which other people face the same daily challenges they do. Stories also can show children lives that are different from their own, in faraway places and times, where people see and do new and unfamiliar things.

Planning and providing enriching story experiences starts with our recognizing very young children as both *being* and *becoming.* That is, what is happening to and with them in the present is as important as what will happen in the future. We don't talk to children, sing, play language games, recite nursery rhymes, and tell and read stories only because we want to prepare children for *future* learning (although happily that is a benefit). We also do these things because we know those experiences enrich children's present lives by helping them to learn, love, and have a joyful time with language.

We choose the most amusing, interesting stories for very young children because they are most likely to provide interesting insights, information, and points of view, giving pleasure in the process. We choose the best and most beautiful books for the same reasons. Doing this well requires us to have specific knowledge of each child, informed by an understanding of what we can typically expect at various ages and developmental stages, and tempered by an awareness of the wide range of individual differences among children.

Stories strengthen the relationships around children

Infants and toddlers are in the early but critical stages of developing their sense of personal identity: "Who am I? Am I a worthwhile person? Do I fit in? Am I lovable?" Young children find answers to these questions in the relationships they have with the important adults in their lives. When the adults who care for them are responsive and loving, children learn to trust that the world is a safe place to explore and that they are loveable and capable people. Stories are inestimably valuable in exciting, entertaining, and establishing the strong emotional bonds between children and adults, which aid in learning, healthy attachment, and development.

Stories weave bright threads of communication and connection through all human relationships. Within their families and communities, stories teach children about who they are and where they come from. Stories also can let children know that they are members of "the human family," and that we all feel the same range of emotions, from stressful to joyful. Stories between peers can bring children together in a mutually pleasant experience, as well as give them common experiences to integrate into their play and conversations.

Stories can also reflect and support the values of inclusion. Children need to find themselves and their important relationships reflected in stories—and this means every child. An inclusive approach to sharing stories is an essential component of good practice. This might entail making books available in children's home languages, giving support for speaking those languages, including images of children who look like them, making accommodations that ensure their full participation in story experiences, as well as bringing stories about or from their home cultures and communities into our programs. Through story experiences, children can explore and be taught to appreciate and respect all the differences and similarities that exist among people.

Stories not only foster caring relationships between adults and children, they are also a powerful tool in forging partnerships between caregivers and families. Children's most powerful learning originates in and reflects their family life, so establishing partnerships with those families should be a central goal of our care. This means respecting each family's values and beliefs, stories, and ways of sharing their stories with their children. It also means helping children make seamless transitions between home and program. Everyone benefits when families and caregivers form trusting relationships and exchange resources and information about the child. Stories bring children and adults together, and they help us forge bonds to maintain those connections.

Stories support children's emerging literacy skills

Children are becoming literate from birth. All the strategies that stimulate, sustain, and respond to infants' and toddlers' language development and their participation as listeners, observers, sound makers, singers, and speakers—in short, all the strategies that nurture a love of stories—are also developing their emerging literacy skills. Infants and toddlers are becoming (and being) literate, first through very early experiences with listening, looking, and vocalizing; and later through their encounters with told stories, books, and environmental text in their everyday lives.

Among the many valuable skills and lessons that children learn from meaningful experiences with stories, both spontaneous and planned, are attentive listening, proper handling of books, and conventions of print. Vocabulary, comprehension, and background knowledge are cultivated through the wise use of stories, too. In the years before primary school, the foundation is laid (or not) for children to become competent speakers, listeners, readers, and writers (Parlakian 2003). When we support children's natural love of stories, we are nurturing dispositions important to learning, including curiosity, enthusiasm, engagement, desire to learn, and sense of fun and pleasure.

Literacy as social justice

For children whose life circumstances are disadvantaged—for example, by family poverty—literacy, especially in the society's dominant language, can be crucial for securing a better future. As former United Nations Secretary-General Kofi Annan stated on International Literacy Day, September 8, 1997, "Literacy is a bridge from misery to hope. It is a tool for daily life in modern society. It is a bulwark against poverty, and a building block of development."

Because they contribute so much to children's developing literacy, access to quality story experiences is a matter of social justice and equity (Feeney & Moravcik 2005; Volk & Long 2005; Cachevki-Williams & Cooney 2006). Providing such experiences in our programs is our first responsibility. We can also acquaint families with what story resources may exist for children under 3 in their community. A surprising number of adults have yet to discover, for example, the incredible resources of public libraries, or they do not realize that libraries have much to offer infants and toddlers.

As literacy expert Mary Jalongo reminds us, "The satisfactions of literature should not be the province of a privileged few. Children are universally entitled to meaningful experiences with memorable books" (2004, 10). Establishing partnerships between families and early childhood education programs can be a giant step toward balancing an inequality of resources.

Stories are not just for children.

As with so much of what we provide to young children, the quality and value of story experiences depend as much on how and why we do what we do as on what we do. When we model reading, writing, speaking, and listening, we powerfully influence and guide children's behavior. One of the most valuable things an early childhood program can do is motivate young children to be and become listeners, speakers, readers, and writers. As children's author Mem Fox reminds us, literacy—just like all of children's learning and development—relies on strong relationships:

> The fire of literacy is created by the emotional sparks between a child, a book, and the person reading. It isn't achieved by the book alone, nor by the child alone, nor by the adult who is reading aloud—it's the relationship winding between the three, bringing them together in easy harmony. (2001, 10)

Finally . . .

Stories are not just for children. Jim Greenman (2008) writes powerfully about the contribution stories make to the life of an early childhood program:

> We share our lives through stories: Stories of day to day events, struggle, outrage, hope, pain, happiness or misery, pleasure, failure, and triumph. Through telling stories, we seek validation and try and find common ground. Stories can promote positive or negative cultural traits: inclusiveness or exclusiveness; innovation or the status quo, suspicion or good will, or sharing or hoarding. . . .

While we do share stories to help children become competent, the main reason for using stories during the early years is to add pleasure and meaning to individual children's lives, the lives of those who share stories with children, and the collective life of a group of children in a program.

Young children who are given the gift of stories, who learn to love them from an early age and enjoy their endless benefits, have received a gift that will last a lifetime, one that provides pleasure in the present and limitless possibilities for the future. It is a gift that is ours to give.

Developmental Milestones, Birth to Age 3	
The child . . .	*The implications for sharing stories are . . .*
Birth to 4 months—Connecting and communicating with others through listening and gazing	
Looks at adults' eyes. Prefers to look at human faces over other shapes or figures	Take time during routines such as bathing for gentle conversations, so that your voice and your facial expressions show your enjoyment of being with her
Has poorly developed vision at birth, able to focus at a distance of only 8–10 inches. By 3 months, can visually follow a moving object. Will study an object placed within his range of vision	Hold the infant close to you; hold objects close. Show him books with one picture or clear photograph on a page
Pays most attention to patterns with a sharp contrast between the design and the background (e.g., brightly colored or black designs on white)	Books should have large, simple designs on a contrasting background (e.g., simple board books that have bold, sharply contrasting illustrations or pictures)
Communicates through sounds (e.g., crying) and reflex actions (e.g., wriggling); by 3 months, sounds include cooing	Acknowledge the infant's communication efforts by responding (e.g., saying reassuringly, "I think you are hungry; it's time for me to feed you")
Responds to high-pitched voices and variations in pitch	Books are less important than human voices are. Rhymes and songs are particularly enjoyable for this age group. Use your voice to keep her listening when you share books or sing songs or rhymes
Pays particular attention to the voice of the primary caregiver; turns his head toward familiar voices	Primary caregivers are the best people to share conversations, songs, and rhymes with very young infants
Starts to smile and laugh around familiar adults	Using words and facial expressions, reinforce these early nonverbal communication efforts (e.g., "Yes, you are a happy baby today" as you smile at her)

The child . . .	The implications for sharing stories are . . .
Listens actively to all the sounds around him, especially speech directed at him	Use *child-directed speech:* elevated pitch, variations in pitch, long pauses, and exaggerated stress on syllables It doesn't matter so much what the story is about; it is the tone of your voice and your face that attracts attention
At birth, can lift her head only briefly when lying on her tummy; by 3 months, can keep her head raised By 3 months, infant can be held upright in your lap without her head flopping over	Hold or place an open book in front of her (if she's on her tummy) or alongside the crib; but not so many that she can't turn away if she becomes overstimulated
Can grasp objects placed in his palm; by 3 months, he explores objects by putting them in his mouth	Provide stiff, cardboard books that are easily cleaned
4 to 8 months—Absorbing and experimenting with sounds, interactions, and movement	
By 8 months, has more control of her gaze and is able to observe more keenly; also develops full color vision and mature distance vision	Verbally point out and label anything that attracts her gaze. Share books with simple color pictures or photographs
Adds consonant sounds to his cooing of vowel sounds. By 7 months, can babble a series of consonants (e.g., "da-da-da-da")	Chant rhymes and repeat his babbles. Name objects as you interact with him (e.g., "Here is your teddy," "Look, a red truck")
Enjoys opportunities to "converse" with adults in a more sustained fashion. Begins to understand that a conversation is about taking turns	Listen and respond to her vocalizations and "talk": child makes a sound, adult makes a sound Smile and speak to show you enjoy these conversations: "Oh, so you want to talk with me today! Well, I like talking with you, too"

The child . . .	The implications for sharing stories are . . .
Continues to be interested in and enjoys being with familiar people	Share simple books, such as concept books, as occasions to share close, warm interactions
Begins to imitate the facial expressions, gestures, and body actions of familiar adults	Imitate his expressions and show your appreciation of his ability to do the same. Play games such as peek-a-boo Hold him so he can see your face or a book when you are sharing stories, songs, or books
Elaborates on the sounds learned a month or so ago. This may take the form of trills and one-syllable exclamations Makes different types of sounds and tones (e.g., loud, soft, high, low)	Repeat sounds back and watch how she imitates your sounds or facial expressions Sing songs and chant rhymes; play simple face games (e.g., "Round and round the garden," which includes tickling under the chin)
By 6–7 months, can sit without support, freeing his hands for grasping and holding objects Still puts everything in his mouth; begins banging and waving objects	Use cloth and vinyl books, which can be grasped easily and are washable
By 8 months, likes to drop and toss objects; can handle objects with more skill to examine and manipulate them	Provide sturdy, chunky board books for exploration. When sharing books with the baby, model how to turn pages, and help her to do this
By 8 months, may begin crawling; often prefers moving about to sitting and examining objects	Put board books where he can reach them

The child . . .	The implications for sharing stories are . . .
8 to 12 months—Remembering and actively exploring	
Understands a lot of what adults say (*receptive speech*), so verbal interactions can be more complex. Still is unable to use much *expressive speech* herself	Share simple stories or talk about events, people, and animals that are familiar (e.g., saying "Daddy's coming" causes her to look toward the door). Provide large, clear pictures and talk about them (e.g., "Look, that's an elephant. It is sooo big! Bigger than your daddy!")
Still babbles, but his sounds start to have the tone and variation of "real" speech, imitating the talk he has heard	Continue to vocalize in response to his babbling. Use nursery rhymes, language plays, and songs to reinforce his interest in sound making
Uses actions as well as vocalizations to communicate (pointing, nodding, making eye contact)	Be expressive when sharing stories and talking. Use face, hand, and body movements to help convey the meaning of your words
By 12 months, will look at the correct picture when an object is named (e.g., "Where's the bear?"); recognizes her own name when spoken	Content of the book becomes important. Share simple books and point to pictures. Encourage her to point to pictures, too. Use her name in a told story
Around 12 months, begins using recognizable words (e.g., *no* and *mama*). Vocalizations are many and often loud	Share stories that use words he can say. Use an expressive voice in your conversations, storytelling, and reading
Around 12 months, starts to show imaginative play behaviors (e.g., "feeding" a teddy bear) May respond to pictures as if they were real (e.g., smacking her lips when looking at a picture of food, patting a picture of a cat)	Introduce a small amount of fantasy or imagination into your stories (e.g., "Teddy says he is very hungry! Do you think he would like to taste some blocks? No? How about some crackers? There, Teddy, was that a good snack?")

The child . . .	The implications for sharing stories are . . .
May begin to search for objects that are hidden from view. Will remember and look for a favorite book to share with you	Play peek-a boo games; introduce simple, sturdy lift-the-flap books; ask questions such as "What might be under this flap?" or "Who is hiding under here?"
Can reproduce sounds from many different languages. Gradually distinguishes the sounds that are used in his home language and culture	When possible, support development of the child's first language by using it for stories and other language experiences
Has increasing control over her hand and finger movements, but coordination is still awkward	Provide books with cardboard pages, which are easy for her to turn; it is still too early for paper pages
Is increasingly mobile. Crawls and enters the early stage of walking Carries around objects; may bring you a book, meaning "Read this"	Provide story spaces that he can freely explore. When the baby shows interest in a book, sit with him and share the book together

12 to 18 months—Imitating and exploring

The child . . .	The implications for sharing stories are . . .
Has better memory. Recognizes familiar language, sounds, objects. Can remember language heard repeatedly in stories and other language experiences Can understand a dramatically accelerating number of words	Share stories with simple refrains or phrases that she might repeat Name objects when she points or (later) asks, "Wha dat?" Share books that label familiar objects or have repetitive storylines (character eats, dresses, sleeps, etc.)
Finds repetition and predictability in daily life reassuring. Is likely to get a different meaning out of a story each time he hears it	Respond to requests for you to read or tell favorite stories again and again. Share stories with familiar events, objects, and characters
Responds to questions with sounds (including words) and gestures	Share books with simple questions that she can respond to (e.g., *Where Is the Green Sheep?* by Mem Fox)

The child . . .	The implications for sharing stories are . . .
By 16 months, may string many nonsense sounds together with tone and pace that sound like sentences By 18 months, may be able to use a number of individual words accurately and begin to say simple, two-word sentences	Respond to his conversation and other attempts to communicate (e.g., "Yes, Davis, you want to ride in the wagon?" in response to his saying, "Me go, me go, dat" as he points to the wagon) Give him unhurried time to respond to your conversation
Practices many motor skills repeatedly to gain mastery and for sheer enjoyment; likes to repeat actions that she sees familiar adults do (e.g., reading a book)	Encourage her to do the actions or movements when you share rhymes, songs, or poems. Provide sturdy books for her to use independently. Recognize that the child's talk when she uses a book independently is her attempt to sound like she is reading
Probably walking; increasingly fascinated with mobility and driven to explore his environment	Stopping for stories may not always appeal to busy walkers and explorers. Sing songs, tell rhymes or poems with lots of actions he can join in as he is moving. Share stories when he is ready to slow down
As mobility improves, may express intense pleasure or interest using her whole body By 18 months, is more likely to sit for lap reading and to express engagement verbally	Encourage her engagement with the story, including clapping, jumping, dancing, demonstrating, or otherwise joining in physically Give her opportunities to hold the book as you read it

18 months to 2 years—Expressing self, making meaning, and discovering

Can enjoy increasingly complex images as his vision acuity improves	Introduce picture books or other images with greater visual detail. Allow his unhurried time to examine them closely
Demonstrates in a variety of ways that she understands a great deal of what is said to her (e.g., can answer questions about familiar objects depicted in books by pointing)	Share books and told stories that include everyday objects she can point to or name

The child . . .	The implications for sharing stories are . . .
Expresses keen interest in everyday events	Use stories about children who accomplish familiar tasks (e.g., drinking from a cup, feeding himself, dressing and undressing). Use his name in stories, songs, or simple rhymes, and relate these stories to his experiences
By age 2, asks questions, sometimes over and over (e.g., "Wha dat? . . . Wha dat?")	Share stories that ask simple questions, such as prediction (e.g., "Who is hiding there?"). Ask your own simple questions as you read a story (e.g., "Did the puppy go home?")
Is a more effective speaker, as her vocabulary grows. Can name many objects and familiar people	Share books and told stories that include everyday objects that the child can point to or name
Imitates adult expressions in speech and words (e.g., "Uh-oh," "No!")	Be expressive when sharing stories or other spoken language experiences
By age 2, uses phrases and simple sentences (e.g., "Daddy goed car," "My book," "No nap")	Continue to allow unhurried time for him to talk and express his needs. Acknowledge his communication efforts and model mature forms (e.g., "Yes, Daddy went in his car")
By age 2, is interested in gender and identity	Share stories about toddlers. Be sure they feature a balance of girls and boys and avoid stereotypes
Engages in more elaborate pretend play with stuffed animals, toy vehicles, dolls. May improvise with objects, using them imaginatively (e.g., moving a block around the floor while making car noises)	Introduce more complex stories with imaginative elements (e.g., *Mr. Gumpy's Motor Car*, by John Burningham)

The child . . .	The implications for sharing stories are . . .
Begins making marks or scribbling as first attempts at communicating in nonverbal ways Understands that signs, symbols, and images can convey messages or tell stories (e.g., "Dat Mommy," as she draws with large circular movements). May enjoy repeating large movements as she draws or paints	Provide daily opportunities for her to draw, paint, and make marks Document her words if she offers what she is drawing (do not force this by continuously asking, "What have you drawn?"). Allow for spontaneous comments Use rhymes when she is drawing or scribbling: "Round and round the pencil goes, where it stops, nobody knows"
Is increasingly able to think and remember in order to solve problems, recall events, make requests, figure things out	Introduce more complex stories, with plots and characters who resolve dilemmas. Ask him to choose which book to read
By age 2, knows generally how books and reading work according to her cultural reading or literacy traditions (e.g., front to back, left to right, etc.)	Give her sturdy books to handle; model book-handling and reading conventions. Introduce books in other languages, especially familiar stories

2 to 3 years—Becoming creative with language

Increasingly enjoys humor (especially slapstick and incongruity) and jokes	Share stories with funny themes or events. Tell simple jokes, which can be stories, too
By age 3, can talk about feelings (e.g., commenting about an illustration "That boy is sad 'cause he's crying"). Is interested in "good"/"bad" behaviors	Help him identify simple feelings expressed in picture storybooks. Ask simple questions about feelings when sharing a story (e.g., "Was the baby bird happy or sad?"). Offer stories in which characters misbehave
Is a more confident communicator. Increasingly uses words and phrases in combination with gestures and other actions	Share stories accompanied by physical actions and action language games
Uses language in original and creative ways (e.g., instead of "mosquito bite," she may say, "squito-mo-bite")	Document her creative language as a sign of her increasing understanding of how language works

The child . . .	The implications for sharing stories are . . .
Can make comparisons, correctly using concepts such as *big/small, in/out,* in response to questions such as "Is the elephant big or small?" Likes to put things in categories	Use concept books as occasions for extended talk about the pictured objects. Share information books to support his increasing understanding of and curiosity about the world
By age 3, asks to hear favorite stories over and over again. Can sing simple favorite songs and will ask for them to be sung	Encourage her to identify favorite stories and songs
Is increasingly confident in his abilities. Has greater capacity for imagination; pretend play is more complex and sustained	Support his efforts as an oral storyteller and in acting out simple stories. Document these storytelling events as important developmental achievements

Encourage an older child to share his favorite stories with peers; provide props such as puppets, large flannel pieces, dress-up materials |
Finds a broader range of stories appealing, due to more life experiences and increased understanding	Share stories that connect with her expressed interests. Story content can be broadened to include unfamiliar places, events, and people/roles
By age 3, understands that pictures and words are symbols for real objects	Read and discuss together a variety of books and other representations in print and pictures. Give her opportunities to "write" stories
Is increasing exponentially the number of words he can use, heavily influenced by his experiences and relationships	Encourage him to dictate stories you write down together. Encourage him to think of new words to familiar songs or rhymes (e.g., "Old Macdonald had a . . . what?")
By age 3, she enjoys telling her own stories about herself or imaginary stories about toys, people she knows, or events. These stories may have a character, a simple sequence, and show some emotional response ("Oh my doggy can't run, my doggy is sick, poor doggy")	Recognize this storytelling skill and support it by extending the story through questions or enriching the language through your comments ("Where will you take your sick doggy?" or "Yes, the dog doctor is a good idea, we call them veterinarians")

Sources: This chart borrows extensively from Schickedanz (1999) and Blakemore & Ramirez (2006). The following additional sources were used: Bredekamp & Copple (1997); Pruitt (2000); Albrecht & Miller (2001); Jalongo (2004); Shelov (2004); Puckett & Black (2007).

Good Books for Infants and Toddlers

The list below represents only a small fraction of the enormous number of good books published for very young children. It includes classics first published in the last century up through those published in 2007. The books come mostly from Australia, the United Kingdom, and the United States, and all are readily available from major booksellers. Many of the books are available in hardback, paperback, and as board books. Some authors have several books listed, but they may well have further publications suitable for very young readers that could be sourced through a bookseller or library.

Many recommended children's book lists are available online. In particular, nonprofit groups that are invested in young children's learning and development often make such lists available to help teachers and families select materials. Reading Rockets (http://www.readingrockets.org/), Book'Em (http://www.bookem-kids.org/), and Books for Kids (http://www.books forkidsfoundation.org) offer some excellent resources for sharing books with children.

The books in this list range from very simple one-word concept books to quite complex storybooks. Some books that might be thought to be appropriate for older children have been included, if families and caregivers have found through experience that some younger children enjoy them, too.

Ahlberg, Janet, & Allan Ahlberg. *Peepo!*

Allen, Pamela. *Mr. McGee* series
   My first 1, 2, 3

Baby Love series. *I like my soft teddy bear*
   I can smile at you
   I feel soft and smooth

Berenstain, Stan, & Jan Berenstain. *Berenstain Bears and the spooky old tree*

Blackstone, Stella. *Bear in a square*

Bodsworth, Nan. *A nice walk in the jungle*

Bowie, C.W. *Busy toes*
   Busy fingers

Bradman, Tony, & Clive Scruton. *A goodnight kind of feeling*

Brown, Margaret Wise. *Goodnight moon*
   The noisy book
   The runaway bunny

Bunting, Eve. *Flower garden*

Burke, Tina. *Sophie's big bed*

Burningham, John. *Mr. Gumpy's motor car*
    Mr. Gumpy's outing

Butler, John. *Can you cuddle like a koala?*
    Hush, little ones
    While you were sleeping
    Who says woof?

Campbell, Rod. *Dear zoo*
    Noisy farm

Carle, Eric. *Does a kangaroo have a mother, too?*
    From head to toe
    My Very First series
    The grouchy ladybug
    The very hungry caterpillar
    The very lonely firefly

Cauley, Lorinda Bryan. *Clap your hands*

Chocolate, Deborah Newton. *On the day I was born*

Cooke, Trish. *Full, full, full of love*

Cowell, Cresida. *What shall we do with the boo-hoo baby?*

Cowen-Fletcher, Jane. *Mama zooms*

Dodd, Lynley. *Hairy MacLary* series

Eck, Kristin. *Colores en mi casa* (*Colors in my house*)
    Opuestos en mi casa (*Opposites in my house*)

Ehlert, Lois. *Color farm*

Falconer, Ian. *Olivia's opposites*

Falwell, Cathryn. *Feast for 10*

Fox, Mem. *Hattie and the fox*
    Possum magic
    Time for bed
    Whoever you are

Fox, Mem, & Judy Horacek. *Where is the green sheep?*

Fuge, Charles. *My dad!*

Gleeson, Libby. *Cuddle time*

Graham, Bob. *Dimity Dumpty: The story of Humpty's little sister*

Gravett, Emily. *Monkey and me*

Gray, Kes. *My mum goes to work*

Hatkoff, Isabella, Craig Hatkoff, & Paula Kahumbu. *Owen and Mzee: The true story of a remarkable friendship*

Hayes, Sarah. *Eat up, Gemma*

Hest, Amy. *Kiss good night*

Hill, Eric. *Spot* series

Hindley, Judy. *The big red bus*

Hoban, Russell. *Frances* series

Hoban, Tana. *Black on white*
    White on black

Holub, Joan. *My first book of sign language*

Hutchins, Pat. *Changes, changes*
    Tidy Titch

Inkpen, Mick. *Is it bedtime Wibbly Pig?*

Joosse, Barbara. *Mama, do you love me?*

Katz, Karen. *Counting kisses*
    Toes, ears, & nose!
    Where is baby's belly button?

Keats, Ezra Jack. *The snowy day*

Kubler, Annie. *Sign and sing along: Twinkle, twinkle, little star*

Lehman, Barbara. *The red book* [wordless picture book]

Lewis, Anthony. *Meal time*

Lewis, Kevin. *Chugga chugga choo choo*

Lionni, Leo. *Let's play*

Lodge, Jo. *My little case of jungle animals*

Lofts, Pamela. *Dunbi the owl*
    How the birds got their colours
    How the kangaroos got their tails

Long, Sylvia. *Hush little baby*

Mackintosh, David. *Same as me*

Martin, Bill, Jr. *Brown bear, brown bear, what do you see?*
    Chicka chicka boom boom
    Panda bar, panda bear, what do you see?
    Polar bear, polar bear, what do you hear?

Masurel, Claire. *Two homes*

McCloskey, Robert. *Blueberries for Sal*
    Make way for ducklings

McCully, Emily Arnold. *Picnic*

McDonnell, Flora. *Splash!*

Merberg, Julie, & Suzanne Rober. *A magical day with Matisse*
    A picnic with Monet
    Dancing with Degas
    Sharing with Renoir

Miller, Virginia. *Eat your dinner!*
     Get into bed! A story about going to sleep
     On your potty!

Morris, Ann. *Bread, bread, bread*

Munsch, Robert. *Love you forever*

Niland, Deborah. *Let's play!*
     When I was a baby

Norling, Beth. *Little brothers are . . .*
     Little sisters are . . .

Oborne, Martine. *One gorgeous baby*

Ormerod, Jan. *Dad's back*
     Messy baby

Oxenbury, Helen. *All fall down*
     Clap hands
     Say goodnight
     Shopping
     Tickle, tickle

Parr, Todd. *The daddy book*
     The family book
     The mommy book
     The peace book

Penn, Audrey. *The kissing hand*

Pienkowski, Jan. *Colours*

Pinkney, Andrea, & Brian Pinkney. *I smell honey*

Piper, Watty. *The little engine that could*

Pitzer, Marjorie W. *I can, can you?*

Prater, John. *Again!*

Priddy, Roger. *Animals*

Prince, April Jones. *What do wheels do all day?*

Rabe, Berniece. *Where's Chimpy?*

Rathmann, Peggy. *Good night, gorilla*

Rotner, Shelley. *Lots of feelings*

Rowe, Jeanette. *Whose house?*
     Whose tail?
     Whose teeth?

Scott, Ann Herbert. *On mother's lap*

Sendak, Maurice. *Where the wild things are*

Seuss, Dr. *The cat in the hat*

Sheehan, Peter. *Plane, train, truck and trolley*

Sieveking, Anthea. *What color?*

Slobodkina, Esphyr. *Caps for sale*

Smee, Nicola. *Sleepyhead*

Stiegemeyer, Julie. *Cheep! Cheep!*

Swain, Gwenyth. *Bedtime*
    Carrying
    Celebrating
    Eating
    Wash up

Tildes, Phyllis Limbacher. *Baby animals black and white*

Venus, Pamela. *Let's feed the ducks*
    Let's go to bed
    Let's have fun

Waddell, Martin. *Owl babies*

Walton, Rick, & Paige Miglio. *So many bunnies: A bedtime ABC and counting book*

Wild, Margaret. *Chatterbox*
    Kiss kiss!
    Little Humpty
    Seven more sleeps
    The little crooked house

Wilkes, Angela. *My first word book*

Willems, Mo. *Knuffle bunny: A cautionary tale*

Williams, Sue. *I went walking*

Williams, Vera B. *"More more more," said the baby*
    Music, music for everyone

Wood, Audrey. *The napping house*
    Silly Sally

Yolen, Jane. *Off we go!*

Zelinsky, Paul O. *Knick-knack Paddywhack*
    The wheels on the bus

Ziefert, Harriet. *Beach party!*

Zolotow, Charlotte. *William's doll*

References

Albrecht, K., & L.G. Miller. 2001. *Infant and toddler development*. Beltsville, MD: Gryphon House.

Annan, K. 1997. *United Nations press release: Secretary-General stresses need for political will and resources to meet challenge of fight against illiteracy*. Online: http://www.un.org/News/Press/docs/1997/19970904.SGSM6316.html.

Anning, A., & A. Edwards. 2006. *Promoting children's learning from birth to five: Developing the new early childhood professional*. Berkshire, England: Open University Press.

Anstey, M., & G. Bull. 2000. *Reading the visual: Written and illustrated children's literature*. Sydney: Harcourt Australia.

Arbuthnot, M.H. 1947. *Children and books*. Chicago: Scott, Foresman and Co.

Armbruster, B., M. Lehr, & J. Osborn. 2003. *A child becomes a reader*. Portsmouth, NH: RMC Research Corporation.

Bardige, B.S., & M. Segal. 2005. *Building literacy with love*. Washington, DC: Zero to Three.

Barton, L.R., & H.E. Brophy-Herb. 2006. Developmental foundations for language and literacy from birth to three years. In *Learning to read the world: Language and literacy in the first three years*, eds. S.E. Rosenkoetter & J. Knapp-Philo, 15–60. Washington, DC: Zero to Three.

Blakemore, C., & C. Ramirez. 2006. *Baby read-aloud basics*. New York: American Management Association.

Bowman, B. 2004. Play in the multicultural world of children: Implications for adults. In *Children's play: The roots of reading*, eds. E. Zigler, D. Singer, & S.J. Bishop. Washington, DC: Zero to Three.

Bredekamp, S., & C. Copple, eds. 1997. *Developmentally appropriate practice in early childhood programs*. Rev. ed. Washington, DC: NAEYC.

Bronfenbrenner, U. 1979. *The ecology of human development*. Cambridge, MA: Harvard University Press.

Burns, M.S., P. Griffin, & C.E. Snow, eds. 1999. *Starting out right: A guide to promoting children's reading success*. Washington, DC: National Academy Press.

Butler, D. 1998. *Babies need books*. Portsmouth, NH: Heinemann.

Cachevki-Williams, K., & M. Cooney. 2006. Young children and social justice. *Young Children* 61 (2): 75–82.

Carter, M. 1994. Finding our voices—The power of telling stories. *Exchange Every Day* (July/August). Online: http://www.childcareexchange.com/eed/.

Centre for Community Child Health. 2004. Reading with young children. *Community Paediatric Review* 13 (1): 1–4.

Clay, M. 2001. *Change over time in children's literacy development*. Auckland, NZ: Heinemann.

Curenton, S. 2006. Oral storytelling: A cultural art that promotes school readiness. *Young Children* 61 (5): 78–89.

Duff, A. 1944. *Bequest of wings: A family's pleasure with books*. New York: Viking Press.

Dyson, A.H. 1994. "I'm gonna express myself": The politics of story in children's worlds. In *The need for story*, eds. A.H. Dyson & C. Genishi. Urbana, IL: National Council of Teachers of English.

Early Childhood Australia. 1999. *Position statements: Language and literacy.* Online: http://www.earlychildhoodaustralia.org.au/position_statements/language_and_literacy.html.

Erickson, K.A., D. Hatton, V. Roy, D.L. Fox, & D. Rennie. 2007. Literacy in early intervention for children with visual impairments: Insights from individual cases. *Journal of Visual Impairment & Blindness* 101 (2): 80–94.

Feeney, S., & E. Moravcik. 2005. Children's literature: A window to understanding self and others. *Young Children* 60 (5): 20–28.

Fox, M. 2001. *Reading Magic.* New York: Harcourt.

Gandini, L., & J. Goldhaber. 2001. *Two reflections about documentation, Bambini—the Italian approach to infant/toddler care.* New York: Teachers College Press.

Greenman, J. 2008. Growing organizational culture: The power of stories. *Exchange Every Day* (May/June). Online: http://www.childcareexchange.com/eed/.

Gregory, E., & C. Kenner. 2003. The out of schooling of literacy. In *Handbook of early literacy*, eds. N. Hall, J. Larson, & J. Marsh. New York: Guilford.

Hawley, T. 2000. *Starting smart: How early experiences affect brain development.* Washington, DC: Zero to Three, and Chicago, IL: The Ounce of Prevention Fund.

Huck, C., S. Hepler, J. Hickman, & B. Kiefer. 2000. *Children's literature in the elementary school*, 7th ed. In *Young children and picture books*, 2d ed., 2004, ed. M.J. Jalongo, 35. Washington, DC: NAEYC.

Jablon, J.R., A.L. Dombro, & M.L. Dichtelmiller. 2007. *The power of observation for birth through eight.* 2d ed. Washington, DC: Teaching Strategies, and Washington, DC: NAEYC.

Jalongo, M.J. 2004. *Young children and picture books.* 2d ed. Washington, DC: NAEYC.

Jones-Diaz, C., & N. Harvey. 2007. Other words, other worlds: Bilingual identities and literacy. In *Literacies in childhood: Changing views, challenging practice*, eds. L. Makin, C. Jones-Diaz, & C. McLachlan, 203–216. Marrickville, NSW: Elsevier Australia.

Juel, C. 2006. The impact of early school experiences on initial reading. In *Handbook of early literacy research*, vol. 2, eds. D.K. Dickinson & S. Neuman, 410. New York: Guilford.

Katz, L., & T. Schery. 2006. Including children with a hearing loss in early childhood programs. *Young Children* 61 (1): 86–95.

Lally, R., & P. Mangione. 2006. The uniqueness of infancy demands a responsive approach to care. *Young Children* 61 (4): 14–20.

Lancaster, L. 2002. Staring at the page: The functions of gaze in a young child's interpretation of symbolic forms. *Educational Administration Abstracts* 37 (2): 143–276.

Long, G.E., & D. Volk, eds. 2004. *Many pathways to literacy: Young children learning with siblings, grandparents, peers and communities.* New York: Routledge Farmer.

Magee, J., & E. Jones. 2004. Leave no grown-up behind—Coming to terms with technology. *Young Children* 59 (3): 13–20.

Makin, L. 2006. Literacy 8–12 months: What are babies learning? *Early Years: An International Journal of Research and Development* 26 (3): 267–277.

Makin, L., & M. Whitehead. 2004. *How to develop children's early literacy—A guide for professional careers and educators.* London: Paul Chapman.

McCain, M., & F. Mustard. 1999. *Early years study: Reversing the real brain drain.* Final Report to Government of Ontario, Toronto, Canada.

McNaughton, S. 2007. Co-constructing expertise: The development of parents' and teachers' ideas about literacy practices and the transition to school. *Journal of Early Childhood Literacy* 1 (1): 40–58.

Milne, R. 2005. Why do we all love stories? *Clearing House: FKA Children's Services Newsletter* 56 (February).

Mitchell, L.C. 2004. Making the most of creativity in activities for young children with disabilities. *Young Children* 59 (4): 46–49.

Neuman, S.B. 2006. Literacy development for infants and toddlers. In *Learning to read the world: Language and literacy in the first three years*, eds. S.E. Rosenkoetter & J. Knapp-Philo, 275–290. Washington, DC: Zero to Three.

Neuman, S.B., C. Copple, & S. Bredekamp. 2000. *Learning to read and write: Developmentally appropriate practices for young children*. Washington, DC: NAEYC.

Paley, V. 2001. *In Mrs. Tully's room: A childcare portrait*. Cambridge, MA: Harvard University Press.

Papadaki-D'Onofrio, E. 2003. Bilinguliasm/multiculturalism and language acquisition theories. *Child Care Information Exchange* September/October: 46–50.

Parlakian, R. 2003. *Before the ABCs: Promoting school readiness in infants and toddlers*. Washington, DC: Zero to Three.

Pruitt, David B., ed. 2000. *Your child: Emotional, behavioral, and cognitive development from birth through preadolescence*. New York: HarperResource.

Puckett, M., & J. Black. 2007. *Understanding infant development*. St. Paul, MN: Redleaf Press.

Purcell-Gates, V. 1996. Stories, coupons, and the TV guide: Relationships between home literacy experiences and emergent literacy experiences. *Reading Research Quarterly* 31 (4): 406–428.

Rinaldi, C. 2004. The relationship between documentation and assessment. *Innovations in Early Education: The International Reggio Exchange* 11 (1): 1–17.

Rinaldi, C. 2006. *In dialogue with Reggio Emilia: Listening, researching and learning*. London: Routledge.

Rochat, P. 2004. Emerging co-awareness. In *Theories of infant development*, eds. G. Bremmer & A. Slater. Oxford, England: Blackwell.

Rogoff, B. 2003. *The cultural nature of human development*. London: Oxford University Press.

Schickedanz, J. 1999. *Much more than the ABCs: The early stages of reading and writing*. Washington, DC: NAEYC.

Seeger, P., & P. Dubois-Jacobs. 2000. *Pete Seeger's storytelling book*. New York: Harcourt.

Shelov, S.P, & R.E. Hannemann. 2004. *Caring for your baby and young child: Birth to age 5*. Rev. ed. New York: Bantam Books.

Shonkoff, J., & D.A. Phillips, eds. 2000. *From neurons to neighborhoods: The science of early childhood development*. A report of the National Research Council. Washington, DC: National Academies Press.

Shore, R. 1997. *Rethinking the brain: New insights into early development*. New York: Families and Work Institute.

Siraj-Blatchford, I., & P. Clarke. 2000. *Supporting identity, diversity and language in the early years*. Berkshire, England: Open University Press.

Smith, F. 2007. Peace building—The power of ECE. *Exchange Every Day* (July/August). Online: http://www.childcareexchange.com/eed/.

Sulzby, E., & W. Teale. 1991. Emergent literacy. In *Handbook of reading research*, vol. 2, eds. R. Barr, M.L. Kamil, P.B. Mosenthal, & P.D. Pearson. New York: Longman.

Volk, D., & S. Long. 2005. Challenging myths of the deficit perspective: Honoring children's literacy resources. *Young Children* 60 (6): 12–19.

Zable, A. 2002. *The Fig Tree*. Melbourne, AU: The Text Publishing Company.

Zambo, D., & C.C. Hansen. 2007. Love, language, and emergent literacy. *Young Children* 62 (3): 32–37.

Zeece, P.D. 2003. The personal value of literature: Finding books children love. *Early Childhood Education Journal* 31 (3): 133–138.

If you like this book, check out these titles from NAEYC!

Young Children and Picture Books (2d ed.)
Mary Renck Jalongo

When you share picture books with young children, you build their lifelong literacy and enjoyment of reading. In beautiful full color, the new edition of this popular book will help you recognize quality in children's literature and illustration and see how to use picture books to best advantage. Lists of recommended books are included. **Item #160**

Secure Relationships: Nurturing Infant/ Toddler Attachment in Early Care Settings
Alice S. Honig

Loving, responsive, and consistent care from primary caregivers is critical to infants and toddlers in establishing attachment relationships. Experienced author Alice Honig distills key points needed to understand and build attachment, encouraging family members and educators to work together to nurture the children in their care. Vital information and sound advice for caregivers—and families, too. **Item #123**

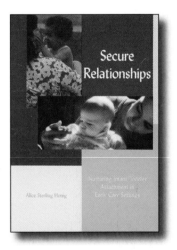